QUICK & HEALTHY MEALS

100+ Recipes Free of Gluten and Refined Sugar

Breakfast and power snacks; smoothies, juices, and drinks;
soups and appetizers; vegetarian entrees; meat-lovers'
entrees; and desserts.

+ Highly nutritious entrees, desserts, and shakes for the whole family!
+ Easy to follow, step-by-step directions

MARIAM KINKLADZE

MINDFUL COOKING

100+ RECIPES FREE OF GLUTEN AND REFINED SUGAR

MARIAM KINKLADZE

MINDFUL COOKING

100+ Highly Nutritious Recipes for Quick and Healthy Meals

Designed by MoneMedia

Photography by Jarret C. Egan & Pooja Malani
Stylist Philippe Grenade

Cover design by Simone Spitzer
Cover photography by Jarret C. Egan
Interior design by Simone Spitzer
Headshot photographer: Joshua Monesson
Interior photos by Jarret C. Egan and Pooja Malani
Jarret C. Egan pages 2, 3, 10, 11, 12, 14, 16, 19, 21, 22, 25, 26, 31, 35, 37, 38, 41, 42, 47, 48, 50, 52, 57, 58, 60, 63, 68, 70, 75, 77, 83, 84, 87, 88, 92, 94, 96, 98, 101, 106, 109, 111, 112, 114, 118, 121, 123, 133, 135, 137, 140, 142, 147, 149, 168, 178, 180, 184, 187, 189, 190, 193, 195, 197, 198, 200, 202, 205, 207, 208, 210, 213, 215, 221, 228
Pooja Malani pages 126, 138, 152, 158, 160, 162, 165

Printed in China

10 9 8 7 6 5 4 3 2 1

First Edition

DEDICATION

This book of recipes is a tribute to my family: **George Papanastasatos,** my partner in healthy consumption, in business, in love, and in life; **my son Lukas,** my "little rocket scientist" and my everything; **and my parents, grandparents, and siblings,** who supported me growing up in Akhmeta and Tbilisi in the Republic of Georgia. It is also a tribute to my history and culture, which undoubtedly affected and enriched my life, and which continue to inspire my recipes today. And of course, it is a tribute to my health—including my battle with endometriosis cysts, anxiety, adrenal fatigue, and my eventual victory after I searched for alternatives, was reminded once again that we are what we eat, and made a change toward a healthier way of living and eating.

TABLE OF CONTENTS

FOREWORD

Mindful Cooking is a lifestyle, not a diet.

The recipes included in this book have been mindfully curated to inspire you to be present while exploring new, innovative ways to eat simply, cleanly, and healthfully. Mindful Cooking is a guide for homemade, wholesome, and delightful recipes for cooks at all levels of expertise, from beginners to experts.

There is no one way of eating that works for all—in order to be truly healthy, we need to stay mindful of our bodies' needs and to accept diet as a tool that can heal, help our bodies recover, and support a healthy lifestyle. I don't believe in strictly following any diet that promises weight loss, skin glow, or digestion healing, but I do believe that all these promises come true when you eat clean, wholesome, and balanced meals, and when you treat each meal as a part of who we are; a lifestyle, not a fad.
Mindful Cooking is for those seeking a healthy, balanced day-to-day life centered on easy-to-follow recipes made with wholesome, locally and organically sourced ingredients.

Each of my recipes calls for highly nutritious ingredients—whole foods that are clean and minimally processed, or not processed at all. This book promotes mainly gluten-free eating. Despite the fact that I am a huge gluten-free-eating advocate, I sometimes indulge on sourdough bread or a slice of pizza made with organic ingredients. In the end, it's all about how our food is prepared—intention followed by execution. Making sourdough bread from scratch at home, for example, is a ritual, and the result is delicious bread that's easier for our bodies to digest.

Dietary Preferences

Everything is about balance in life. Whether you are a vegan, a vegetarian, a flexitarian, or a meat-lover, it's all about finding the right balance for your body. And whatever lifestyle you follow, for true wellness, don't deprive your body, mind, or spirit by indulging in harmful stimulants.

I don't consume meat often—it is a personal preference—but I do love to prepare delicious meat dishes during family gatherings, especially following traditional recipes from my childhood using only 100 percent grass-fed meat. If you are a seafood lover, I recommend choosing sustainably wild-caught seafood. I love pasture-raised eggs. Goat's milk and goat cheese are my absolute favorite dairy. When it comes to cow's milk, I will only recommend organic dairy from A2/A2 cows.

P.S. If you are dealing with a specific health issue, you need to see a doctor. This book is not intended to replace professional medical advice.

Enjoy the recipes!

Love,
Mariam

INTRODUCTION

My roadmap from illness back to good health began with a turn toward healthy eating. I've experienced firsthand how eating healthfully and mindfully can dramatically improve our overall well-being, and I've also learned that just because food is "healthy" doesn't mean it can't be delicious. During my battle with a myriad of health issues, as I searched for alternative methods of healing, I was reminded that we are what we eat, and I learned that in many cases, the healthier choices not only added to my body's overall health, but also tasted even better than the originals. Wholesome, delicious, and nutritious food won't solve every ill, but it's certainly a huge step forward as it helps our bodies and minds work in a healthier, more energetic, and more focused manner—and taking this one step forward will make your remaining steps that much easier. Read on for more on my own personal journey to health, or go ahead and skip right to the recipes to begin taking your first step forward!

I was born and raised in the Republic of Georgia, in a small town named Akhmeta located in the region of Kakheti. Akhmeta was formed in 1945 when two neighboring villages, separated by vast fields of grass, decided to merge. Residential and commercial development expanded over the grasslands to unify the town; however, portions of the fields were preserved and still remain in their natural habitat to this very day. Many of my childhood memories involve nature—running through fields in a game of tag, climbing my favorite apple-picking tree, and visiting a nearby vineyard with my family. There are a great many vineyards in the Katheti region, where wine-making is the main source of income, and most families in my hometown make their own jam or purchase it from small local businesses. As a matter of fact, the local walnut jam, which uses pesticide- and chemical-free nuts, is famous across the entire Republic. Residents of Akhmeta still snack on dried fruit made in their own homes as well, usually flattened and rolled up or combined with nuts and placed in square molds. That's how I was raised—with food made from fresh and mostly organic ingredients. I have fond memories of helping my mom come up with recipes for dinner, and of choosing the fruit and nut combinations for our monthly jam and dried fruit snacks!

My love for cooking and baking began as a young girl observing my mother in action— humming her favorite songs while decorating the edge of a pie with her fork. I especially loved when my mom turned on the radio while we were cooking. If a song that she liked came on, I would encourage her to turn up the volume and start singing or dancing in the kitchen. I knew that if my father came home from work at that moment, she would serenade him or force him to dance with her. Those were the moments I loved, and I soon realized that cooking, and especially baking, had the same positive effect on me as it did on my mother.

My grandmother says I was only three when I declared myself a chef and refused to play with toy food. Apparently, I cried until my mother let me become her "assistant chef" and help prepare the real dinner. My family jokes that they originally created various tasks simply to appease me; however, throughout the years, they came up with scaffolded, age-appropriate tasks that also fit my definition of "assistant chef!" I only remember a handful of my earliest tasks—stirring with mommy at age three, stirring alone at four, washing the lettuce, kneading the dough, and so on—but by the age of eight, I had begun experimenting with my own recipes and documenting the results. I quite admire the extent to which my family truly respected and honed my declared passion at such a young age. I hope I can support my son in this same way—although his current dream is to become a rocket scientist!

Making supermarket lists of the ingredients I needed for my new recipes was easy, but convincing my mother to buy them for me was a bit more challenging. I also still cringe at the memory of my first pie exploding in the oven. I soon realized that in addition to my creative recipe ideas, I needed to learn some more basics. I started observing and assisting any neighbor who would allow me into their kitchen, and watching others, I quickly learned the "dos" and "don'ts" of cooking and baking a variety of meals, from appetizers and entrees to pastries and other desserts. By age nine, I was quite successful with my new recipes and wanted to share them with the whole world—but I decided to start with my own small neighborhood.

Over time, I proved to my parents and siblings that cooking was not just a hobby for me, but a true passion. Their curiosity regarding what I would make next inspired me to keep things fresh, so whether I was inventing a completely original dish or paying my respects to a tried-and-true Georgian classic, I always tried to add my own little twist to every recipe. By the time I was twelve, I had perfected my favorite original desserts, written out my own recipes and menus, and was taking requests from family members and neighbors—and at last, I had been given the title of "family baker!"

I recently found my old little notebook full of recipes, with tiny illustrations of every meal. My handwriting was awful, and the book is full of stains, but it nonetheless serves as a reminder of my Georgian heritage and my childhood passion—and as an inspiration to continue experimenting and developing new recipes!

Growing up in Georgia, we generally enjoyed straight-from-the-farm ingredients that didn't include pesticides, steroids, or chemicals of any kind. Our milk and eggs originated from our own happy chickens and well-treated cows. In other ways, however, living in Georgia had a detrimental effect on my body. At times we would have dirty tap water, and while it made everyone sick for days at a time, it often affected me for weeks or even months after. I would deal with intense pain, bloating, and often vomiting, which I blamed on a weak immune system, and which doctors simply dismissed as being trivial or all in my head. I later learned that after several years of periodically ingesting this water, much of my liver was damaged and my stomach lining had mostly deteriorated.

Eventually, I moved to the United States to pursue greater job opportunities, follow my dream, and make it a reality. Here in the United States, everything is possible. And yet, every country around the world has its own problems that can affect our mental and physical health. While I was following my dream in America, at some point it became easier and cheaper for me to choose premade food and to abandon my old love of cooking and baking. This was my lifestyle for many years, until I realized I had paid a price: eight years after moving to the United States, I found my old health issues re-surfacing in a much more serious way. My digestion had worsened, my liver was enlarged, and soon it was impossible for me to eat food that was processed at all, and even food with dairy or gluten ingredients left me with severe pain and discomfort.

In addition to constant nausea and an upset stomach, my doctor found that I had an ovarian endometrial cyst and recommended invasive surgery to combat it. Thankfully my partner, George Papanastasatos, researched alternate treatments and found that there were other options that had worked successfully for women in my position. We decided to try an alternative treatment before resorting to surgery, and enlisted the help of a holistic doctor. My diet, which I had largely ignored for years, became restricted to only raw, gluten- and dairy-free, organic, and non-GMO foods in order to alkaline and detox my body. Additionally, I began ingesting a variety of herbs, some that I had researched myself and others that had been recommended by an herbalist. After following the diet for only a couple of months, I found great improvement to my health. Not only was I able to avoid surgery, but I also found myself cyst-free and pregnant! My stomach also healed, and I learned how it felt to live without throwing up twice a week or constantly suffering from an upset stomach.

Healing is a process that, even after six years, I am still learning every day, as I continue to work toward healing other issues such as adrenal fatigue and anxiety. One doctor told me that my nervous system is damaged from my past infection; another said that I have fibromyalgia and would have to take medicine for the rest of my life. But after finding an alternative to curing my cyst without surgery—a blessing that left me feeling healthy and pregnant—I continue to look for other means to a healthy end. Of course, medicine is necessary when dealing with infections, and often surgery is simply unavoidable, and I feel lucky to have amazing doctors that I can count on in those circumstances. But whenever I can avoid putting my body under the stress that surgery and medications can cause, I've chosen to find alternatives, and I have managed to live a much less painful life by making the right food choices and enjoying yoga and meditation on a daily basis. And I am not alone: research continues to show the importance of what we ingest and its effect on our bodies.

After this incredible journey that we experienced, my partner George and I realized that we had come to view food in a completely different way. We had developed such a passion for this holistic approach to food, which had saved me from removing my ovaries and left us with our beautiful son Lukas, that we decided we needed to share our experience. We decided to focus our efforts on one of the most important foods that had become a staple in our diet: tigernuts. These are filled with iron, potassium, and fiber and have been found to be helpful for people with digestive disorders, yet they are not well-known in the United States. When we realized the power of this superfood, we made it our mission to help spread the word of this nutrient-rich tuber in order to help others around the world experience the health benefits that I did—and thus, our food brand was soon born under the name Gemini Superfoods.

My healthy-eating journey has improved my physical and mental health and allowed me to live a pain-free and happy life, as well as to regain my love of cooking and baking and begin creating new and mindful healthy recipes to enjoy. I have combined these passions to bring you this book, in an effort to spread the word that healthy, nutritious food can be life-changing—and still be delicious and easy to make!

Mariam Kinkladze

USEFUL TIPS FOR BEGINNING BAKERS

TIP 1: Parchment Paper vs. Greasing
Although greasy pans bring back fond memories of my early days as a baker with my mom, the reality of dealing with the mess and oily residue overrides my nostalgia. Parchment paper is one of my favorite discoveries. Not only do cookies and other pastries slide right off a parchment-lined pan, but the post-baking scrubbing is also reduced to zero. That being said, I have friends who still regularly use the good old-fashioned grease-and-dust method.

TIP 2: Electric Mixer vs. Hand Mixing vs. Food Processor
When the time comes to mix your ingredients together, in most cases I recommend using an electric mixer or food processor to save time and energy and result in a more consistent mixture. But if you do not have an electric mixer available, feel free to use a large spoon or rubber spatula, or for looser mixtures, you can also use a big fork and beat the ingredients together just as you would beat eggs, if you prefer. For cookie and pastry doughs, some people even skip the utensils altogether and use gloved hands to mix all their ingredients. Whatever your preference, make sure to follow any specifics in the recipe to avoid overbeating or damaging delicate ingredients. So while it's fine to substitute a little elbow grease if you don't have an electric mixer, don't use an electric mixer if the recipe tells you to fold the ingredients together with a spoon!

TIP 3: How to Make a Flax Egg
One of the most difficult aspects of plant-based baking is getting the ingredients to bind correctly without using eggs. Flax eggs can be a game changer in solving this problem—with flax eggs, your batter will come together just as well it would using chicken eggs! So how do you make these magical eggs? Either grind up some flaxseed or purchase pre-ground flaxseed meal, combine 1 tablespoon of the ground flaxseed and 3 tablespoons of hot water in a bowl, and let it sit for 5 to 10 minutes in the fridge. That's it! Within 5 to 10 minutes the mixture will become gelatinous and can be used to replace one normal egg.

TIP 4: Use Room-Temperature Ingredients
Though it might seem easier to take ingredients straight from the

refrigerator and incorporate them into your recipe, it actually makes things much more difficult. For example: say you are supposed to mix your butter and sweetener until thoroughly combined. Cold butter is nearly impossible to get to a smooth texture, even with a stand mixer. If your butter is soft and at room temperature, creaming it to a smooth texture or combining it with another ingredient will be much easier to do. The best way to do this is to let your cold ingredients sit on your countertop until soft. Sure, it might take longer to wait for your ingredients to get to room temperature, but trust me, it will save you a huge hassle later when trying to combine them!

TIP 5: Dropping Dough vs. Rolling with Your Hands
Although "dropping dough" may sound like slapping a pile of money on the table, in cookie-baking it actually means using a spoon to scoop up a tablespoon of dough and then using another spoon to push it onto the prepared baking sheet (you can also do this with a cookie scoop, if you have one). After the dough has been dropped onto the baking sheet, I recommend using a fork or your hands to flatten the dough balls down so they cook more evenly—because the cookies in this book are vegan and grain-free, they won't spread into a traditional cookie shape otherwise.

For a better handle on the dough or for more uniformly-shaped cookies, lather your hands in olive oil and form balls of dough using your hands. Next, flatten the balls a bit between your palms and place on the sheet. A cookie scoop would also work if that's your preference.

Whichever method you choose, make sure to place the cookies 2 inches apart on the baking sheet so they have room to spread while they cook!

TIP 6: Know Your Oven
Once your batter or dough is ready, it's easy to want to place your food in the oven and forget about it, but it's important to remember that your job isn't done once you close that oven door. Recipes often include directions you'll need to follow while your food is cooking. Plus, every oven is different, so it's important to learn how yours functions so that you can make adjustments as needed. Your oven probably has hot spots that reach a higher temperature and cook food faster than other parts of the oven. To combat this, a recipe might call for you to rotate the baking pan halfway through cooking. Make sure to follow these directions so your food doesn't cook unevenly. In addition, some ovens run hot or cold. What this

means is that even if you preheat your oven to 425 degrees, your oven might actually be at 400 or 450 degrees instead. The best way to find out how accurate your oven's temperature is is to buy an oven-safe thermometer and go by that when preheating your oven, rather than using the built-in temperature gauge.

TIP 7: Cooling after Baking

After all the effort of making your baked goods, it's tempting to try your treats straight out of the oven. Don't worry, we all feel that way sometimes! But it's best to wait just a little longer, because letting baked goods rest allows them to finish cooking and makes it easier for them to release from the pan without sticking.

For most recipes, I recommend letting your food rest and cool not on its baking pan, but rather on a cooling rack. A wire cooling rack allows air to circulate all around the baked goods (including underneath!) and helps them cool much faster than they would on the still-hot pan. You can easily find an inexpensive cooling rack at most big-box stores and even at some grocery stores. If you don't have a cooling rack, you can also transfer the food to a room-temperature plate. It won't cool as quickly as it would on a cooling rack and air won't circulate underneath, but transferring your goodies off the pan will still cool them—and help you taste-test them—a little quicker!

GLOSSARY OF BAKING TERMS

Baking can be tricky when you're first starting out—especially gluten-free or grain-free baking. In my opinion it's much harder to bake than to cook, because baking requires precise ingredient measuring and careful attention to the recipe instructions. It is imperative to carefully review the recipe before you start baking, and it's essential to know what the baking terms mean in order to avoid having your recipe turn out a failure. Consider this section your baking-recipe dictionary!

Boil To heat a liquid until large, constant bubbles appear.

Combine To mix or blend multiple ingredients in order to create an evenly-distributed mixture. Combining can be done by hand, with a food processor or blender, or with a mixer, depending on the recipe.

Cream To mix butter (or another fat) and a sweetener (maple syrup, coconut sugar, etc.) together into a paste before adding other ingredients. This can be done by hand or with a mixer.

Cooling Rack A metal rack that allows air to flow around baked goods in order to decrease cooling time. Also called a Wire Rack.

Dice To cut a food into small, equal-sized cubes. Many cooks are confused by the difference between dicing and chopping: Dicing refers to cutting food into smaller, more uniform cubes, while the word "chop" is usually used for larger pieces.

Dot To lightly sprinkle an ingredient evenly into a batter or on top of a dish.

Drop To scoop a tablespoon of dough or batter and push it onto the baking sheet using a second spoon.

Dust To lightly sprinkle a dry ingredient, such as flour or sugar, onto a baking sheet or pan to prepare it, or to lightly sprinkle an ingredient onto a finished dish as a topping.

Flour To prepare a baking sheet, pan, or cooking surface by covering in a thin layer of flour. This helps to prevent food from sticking.

Fold To combine ingredients in a more delicate fashion than mixing. A spoon or spatula is used to move the batter from the bottom to the top of the bowl, folding it over the newly added ingredient, then the process is repeated from all angles until the ingredient is equally distributed into the mixture.

Garnish Ingredients that are placed on top of or around a finished food in order to provide added color or flavor.

Grease To prepare a baking sheet or pan for cooking by covering the inside in a thin layer of fat, such as butter or oil. This helps prevent food from sticking.

Knead A way to mix all the ingredients until they form a dough. Kneading can be done by hand or in a stand mixer. If you are using the traditional method and kneading with your hands, put the dough on a floured surface, press and stretch with the heel of your hand, fold it over, and repeat over and over until the dough is smooth.

Line To prepare a baking sheet or pan by placing parchment paper on the bottom. This helps prevent the food from sticking.

Mince To cut food as small as possible; food that is minced should be even smaller than food that is diced.

Mix The most common term for combining ingredients. It can be used to refer to many methods, including stirring with a spoon or mixing with a handheld electric mixer or stand mixer.

Pare To cut off the outer layer of an ingredient or food. Usually done with a small, sharp knife fittingly called a paring knife.

Peel Refers to either the outer layer of a food (such as an orange), or the process of taking off the outer layer (such as peeling an orange).

Pit Refers to either the stone in the middle of a fruit (such as a cherry or a date), or the process of removing the stone, usually with a knife or pitting device.

Preheat To warm the oven or stove to the correct temperature before you are ready to cook or bake. This will save you cooking time, and is especially important for baked goods that require the right temperature to rise properly.

Parchment Paper A heat-resistant, nonstick paper that is used to line baking sheets.

Roll To cover a piece of dough in a dry ingredient (such as sugar) by literally rolling the dough in the ingredient until the entire outside of the dough ball is covered.

Sauté To pan-fry an ingredient quickly with a small amount of light oil on the stovetop.

Scald To heat a liquid to just below the boiling point. A liquid is scalding when it is bubbling around the edges but has not yet hit a full rolling boil.

Shred To separate a food into thin, separate pieces, either by hand or using a utensil.

Sift To pass a dry ingredient, such as sugar or flour, through a sieve in order to reduce clumps and make the ingredient lighter.

Simmer To heat a liquid to a temperature just below the boiling point. A liquid is simmering when there are small bubbles reaching the surface every few seconds.

Soften To allow an ingredient to reach room temperature to soften its texture; usually used in reference to butter.

Stir To use a spoon to lightly mix a batter or group of ingredients by swirling the spoon around the bowl until the ingredients are appropriately combined.

Toss To combine ingredients by lightly lifting and dropping them back into the bowl (for example, tossing a salad to distribute the dressing evenly throughout the bowl).

Whip The process of beating ingredients together, using a utensil called a whisk, to thoroughly combine and add air to the mixture.

Wire Rack See Cooling Rack.

Zest To scrape or cut the outer skin from citrus fruits such as lemons, limes, or oranges. The easiest way to zest fruit is with a zester, or you can use a sharp knife to slice thin pieces of peel from the fruit.

INGREDIENTS

Here are a few of my favorite ingredients that have helped me learn to love natural and clean food. Having these core items in your kitchen pantry will encourage you make more meals from scratch, which is both healthier and tastier.

Gluten-Free and Vegan Flours and Powders

Tigernut Flour: Despite its name, tigernut flour contains no nuts; it actually comes from a root vegetable. This flour is a great substitute for white flour in both cooking and baking, as it produces similar results in taste and consistency and actually rises during baking. It is high in fiber and in natural sugars, which means you can reduce the amount of sweeteners you use alongside it. Our paleo-ancestors relied heavily upon this super-root, which comprised up to 80 percent of their diet. High in fiber, iron, potassium, protein, magnesium, zinc, and vitamins E and C, this nut-free and gluten-free flour is invigorating and even hydrating to our bodies.

Arrowroot Flour: One of the earliest domesticated plants, arrowroot has been used as food for over 10,000 years. Arrowroot flour is extracted from the plant in a more natural way than other starches like cornstarch. It can be used as a thickener when combined with water to make a slurry, and it works well as a baking flour and in frying to make dishes crispier.

Tapioca Flour: Also known as tapioca starch, this starchy ingredient is made by crushing the pulp of the cassava root and is part of the diet of over 500 million people. It is another great baking flour and thickener. It contains almost no sugar or fat and has a neutral flavor and soft texture that is quite similar to grain flour.

Oat Flour: Ground from whole oats, oat flour is high in fiber and has been shown to help decrease high cholesterol. To create oat flour at home, you can pulse oats in a food processor or blender until they are the consistency of a powder.

Cacao Powder: Though they come from the same tree, cacao powder and cocoa powder are quite different. Cacao powder is the raw byproduct of the cacao fruit, while cocoa powder is subjected to much more processing. Filled with antioxidants, cacao powder can make tasty chocolate brownies, smoothies, and more.

Matcha Powder: Matcha is prepared by grinding dried green tea leaves into a distinctive green powder. Whereas to make regular green tea, the leaves are steeped in hot water and then removed, using matcha means using and eating the tea leaves. This allows for the entirety of the natural vitamins, fiber, antioxidants, and other nutrients to be ingested. It has a great, unique flavor, and because it is made from green tea leaves, it even contains caffeine!

Coconut Flour: Due to its sweet and savory flavor, coconut flour is an excellent choice for baking and a wonderful alternative to wheat flour, specifically in paleo, grain-free, and gluten-free recipes. Coconut flour has many health benefits, especially related to the digestive tract. It is high in fiber, and a wonderful substitute for anyone aiming to lose weight while still remaining balanced and healthy.

Cassava Flour: This flour is made from the root of the cassava plant, also known as yucca, which is gluten-, grain-, and nut-free, as well as vegan, vegetarian, and paleo. It stands out for being high in both starch and carbohydrates, making it a hearty addition to any meal, while simultaneously soft in texture and mild in taste, allowing it to soak up any flavor and be used in a variety of dishes. Cassava flour is an excellent replacement for wheat flour, and is regularly enjoyed in gluten-free and grain-free baking and cooking.

Sweeteners

Maple Syrup: Maple syrup is an amazing sweetener, which is why you'll find it in a lot of the recipes in this book. It is my go-to sweetener for baking, and of course, pure maple syrup is essential for drizzling over pancakes and waffles.

Medjool Dates: I consider dates to be nothing less than magical sweeteners. You can create a date paste by soaking and pitting dates and blending or processing them, then use the paste not only to sweeten dishes and desserts but to thicken batters as well. They taste a lot like caramel, and I also keep them in my house for a great grab-and-go snack.

Maple Sugar: Made from pure maple syrup, maple sugar gives you all the benefits and flavors of maple syrup in a granulated or powdered texture.

Coconut Sugar: Though I prefer using maple sugar in my recipes, coconut sugar is the much more cost-effective option. It contains more vitamins and minerals than refined sugar and also contains inulin, a fiber that is known to boost gut health.

Agave Nectar: A vegan alternative to honey, agave nectar is quite sweet and can be used in beverages and in cooking and baking. As with honey, much less agave nectar is needed than refined sugar to reach the same level of sweetness.

Honey: Honey is my favorite sweetener alternative for tea and raw desserts. I love drizzling honey on pancakes as well, and even drizzle it over gluten-free or sourdough toast to enjoy for breakfast or as a snack.

Oils and Butters

Olive Oil: Olive oil is rich in monounsaturated fats and antioxidants, which means it has many health benefits, particularly for the heart. It also has anti-inflammatory properties, which is helpful for those struggling with cancer, diabetes, arthritis, and obesity. It lowers blood pressure and protects the body from "bad" cholesterol, and is even thought to combat Alzheimer's disease.

Coconut Oil: Cold-pressed coconut oil is ideal for baking or cooking, where it's a good substitute for butter or oil. Coconut oil is also full of vitamins that are great for your hair and skin. It's used as an ingredient in many skincare products, but you can also apply any pure coconut oil on your skin to make it very smooth. Cold-pressed coconut oil is made from the coconut meat. The fresh coconut meat is grated, dried, and pressed at varying degrees of pressure and temperature. Add this powerhouse ingredient to your pantry if you haven't already—you won't regret it.

Tahini: Tahini is made from ground sesame seeds and has a deep and nutty flavor. It can be used in anything from dips and salad dressings to cookies and stir-fry recipes.

Vegan Butter: Vegan butter comes in multiple brands you can now get in your local grocery store. It is usable and tasty in both baking and cooking, and can also be used as a spread just like dairy-based butter.

Coconut Butter: Coconut butter is a pure coconut-flavored spread that can be used in a variety of ways, both cooked and uncooked. Unlike coconut oil, it is made by grinding coconut flesh, which means all the nutrients and fiber are retained in the spread.

Almond Butter: Almond butter is a great spread that can be used like peanut butter and is filled with healthy nutrients, including vitamin E, calcium, fiber, magnesium, healthy fats, and more.

Sunflower Butter: Sunflower butter can be purchased or made at home by blending or processing water-soaked sunflower seeds to a smooth paste texture. This spread has more iron, vitamin E, and other nutrients than peanut butter.

Cashew Butter: Like some of the other nut butters listed here, cashew butter is high in iron and magnesium. Cashew butter also has less fat than peanut and other nut butters.

Seeds

Sunflower Seeds: Sunflower seeds can be used in a variety of ways, from baking and cooking with them to having a handful for a quick afternoon snack. They contain protein, vitamin E, and magnesium, among other nutrients.

Pumpkin Seeds: Whether you're purchasing your seeds at the grocery store or roasting them at home, pumpkin seeds are a great source of zinc and protein.

Flax Seeds: Not only does flaxseed contain fiber and omega-3 essential fatty acids, but it also can be used as a replacement for eggs in baking recipes.

Chia Seeds: The secret to chia seeds is in the name: chia is the Mayan term for "strength." They're filled with protein, fiber, antioxidants, and more fantastic nutrients.

Sesame Seeds: Sesame seeds are filled with fiber, calcium, vitamins B6 and E, and other nutrients that help improve digestion. They contribute a tasty, nutty crunch to salads, cookies, and more.

Hemp Seeds: Hemp seeds can be consumed raw, cooked, or roasted, and they have even more protein than chia seeds and flax seeds.

Nuts

Pine Nuts: Pine nuts contain numerous nutrients and high amounts of protein. If you are allergic to pine nuts, you can substitute pistachios in any recipes that call for them.

Cashews: These nuts contain magnesium and copper, which can help keep the bones, skin, and hair healthy.

Walnuts: Walnuts are higher in antioxidants than most other nuts; they can also help promote gut health and lower your risk for type 2 diabetes.

Almonds: On top of their good taste and versatility, almonds also contain fantastic amounts of nutrients, even in small servings, including high amounts of fiber, protein, manganese, and vitamin E.

Pecans: Pecans have the highest amount of fat per serving compared to all the other nuts in this list, but don't let that scare you away! Pecans are filled with healthy fats and have only low amounts of unhealthy saturated fats. They also contain vitamin E, protein, and minerals like copper and manganese.

Vegetables

Tigernuts: Edible tubers that are filled with iron, potassium, and fiber, tigernuts have been cultivated and eaten for thousands of years, and have been found to help people with digestive disorders.

MY FAVORITE MUST-HAVE KITCHEN TOOLS AND EQUIPMENT

Here are the kitchen tools I use day in and day out to make my life easier. The items on this list will keep you organized and ready to bake or cook anytime so much more easily and efficiently.

High-Speed Blender and Food Processor

I use my food processor to make soups, dips, and homemade milks, and my high-speed blender to make smoothies and some dips as well. These are my go-to pieces of equipment, and I use them every day. It's a life-changer to have a good food processor—every family should have one.

Pots and Pans

I love using high-quality stainless-steel pans and pots for everyday cooking. Stainless steel is easier to clean than cast iron, and is not as heavy. In addition, you can store food overnight safely in stainless-steel pots and pans, and they are completely dishwasher-safe. Having a good pan makes food taste better.

Nut-Milk Bags or Cheesecloth

Both nut-milk bags and cheesecloth are great for homemade nut, oat, seed, or root milks. They can be used to strain pulp out of homemade milks, and are reusable—just wash or rinse right after you use them to avoid letting the pulp dry on the cloth. Nothing is better than making your own fresh, plant-based milk. If you've never done so, I highly recommend that you give it a try.

In addition to my favorite tools above, here is the list of must-have tools you'll need to make all the recipes in this book. These items are essential for every home cook and baker.

+ Baking sheets
+ Cookie Sheet
+ Loaf Pan
+ Muffin Liners
+ Muffin Pan
+ Pie Plate
+ Pizza Pan
+ Rectangular Baking Pan
+ Round Cake Pan
+ Square Baking Pan

+ Skillet
+ Chef's Knife
+ Citrus Juicer
+ Hand Mixer/Stand Mixer
+ Kitchen Scissors
+ Measuring Cups
+ Measuring Spoons
+ Metal Spatula
+ Parchment Paper
+ Paring Knife

+ Rolling Pin
+ Slotted Spoon
+ Stainless-Steel Whisk
+ Wire Rack
+ Vegetable Spiralizer
+ Wooden Spoon
+ Zester

 # BREAKFAST AND BAKED GOODS FOR ANYTIME

Active time: 10 minutes
Total time: 40 minutes
Makes: 18 muffins

This blackberry muffin recipe is sure to be a hit at any gathering. I love eating them so much that I usually can't even wait for them to cool down! These are seriously delicious and better than bakery-style gluten-free muffins. But if you want to avoid burning the roof of your mouth, try to have more patience than me!

BLACKBERRY MUFFINS

INGREDIENTS

3 3/4 cups tigernut flour

1 cup tapioca flour

1/2 cup coconut milk powder

2 tablespoons lemon zest
(from 1 lemon)

1 tablespoon arrowroot powder

1 tablespoon flaxseed meal

1 1/2 teaspoons aluminum-free baking powder

1/2 teaspoon baking soda

1 1/3 cups maple syrup

3/4 cup unsweetened apple-sauce

2/3 cup coconut oil, softened to room temperature

1/2 cup hot water

3 tablespoons vanilla extract

8 ounces blackberries, fresh or frozen and thawed

DIRECTIONS

1. Preheat the oven to 350°F. Line two 12-cup muffin tins with paper liners, or grease with coconut oil.

2. In a large mixing bowl, combine the tigernut flour, tapioca flour, coconut milk powder, lemon zest, arrowroot powder, flaxseed meal, baking powder, and baking soda and stir to mix well. In a separate large bowl, combine the maple syrup, applesauce, coconut oil, hot water, and vanilla extract and whisk until well blended. Pour the wet ingredients into the dry ingredients and mix with a spoon or electric mixer until smooth. Fold in the blackberries until they are evenly distributed throughout the batter.

3. Pour the batter into the prepared muffin tins to fill each well three-quarters full. Bake for 30 to 35 minutes, or until a toothpick inserted in the center of a muffin comes out clean. Transfer to a cooling rack and let the muffins cool for 15 minutes before serving.

+ Gluten-Free
+ Grain-Free
+ Refined Sugar-Free
+ Plant-Based
+ Soy-Free,

Active time: 10 minutes
Total time: 35 minutes
Makes: 12 muffins

These gluten-free chocolate chip muffins are simple to make, and they literally melt in your mouth. Once you taste their chocolate chip–vanilla goodness, I promise you'll be making them all year 'round! For a completely plant-based version, you can replace the eggs with flax eggs and the milk with water, and use vegan chocolate chips.

CHOCOLATE CHIP MUFFINS

INGREDIENTS

3 large eggs, lightly beaten (or 3 flax eggs, for a vegan version; see step 2.)

3/4 cup milk (or water, for a vegan version)

1/3 cup coconut oil

2 tablespoons vanilla extract

1 1/4 cups tigernut flour

3/4 cup coconut sugar

1/4 cup coconut flour

1/4 cup arrowroot flour

1 teaspoon baking soda

Pinch of sea salt

3/4 cup chocolate chips made with coconut sugar (or vegan chocolate chips, for a vegan version)

DIRECTIONS

1. Preheat the oven to 350°F. Line a 12-cup muffin tin with paper liners, or grease with coconut oil.

2. For the vegan version, create 3 flax eggs by mixing 3 tablespoons flaxseed meal with 9 tablespoons water. Transfer to the fridge and let rest for 15 to 30 minutes to thicken. (Skip this step if you are not making the vegan version.)

3. In a large bowl, combine the eggs or flax eggs, milk or water, coconut oil, vanilla extract, tigernut flour, coconut sugar, coconut flour, arrowroot flour, baking soda, and sea salt and whisk together until smooth. Carefully fold in the chocolate chips, and mix gently until well combined.

4. Pour into the prepared muffin tin, filling each cup three-quarters full. Bake for 25 minutes for the regular version or 35 minutes for the vegan version, or until a toothpick inserted in the center of a muffin comes out clean. Allow to cool in the pan for 10 minutes, then remove to cool completely.

+ Gluten-Free
+ Grain-Free
+ Refined Sugar-Free
+ Plant-Based (Option)
+ Soy-free

Active time: 10 minutes
Total time: 35 minutes
Makes: 12 muffins

Make your weekend more fun with these delicious seed muffins. I love baking on the weekends when I have more time to make breakfast, and these sweet superfood-packed seed muffins are a staple in my life. They are nutritionally dense and work equally well for breakfast or dessert. Try them once and you will love them forever.

POWER SEED MUFFINS

INGREDIENTS

1/3 cup goji berries

1 cup pureed orange (from about 1 medium orange; peeled and pureed in a food processor)

3 large eggs

3/4 cup organic goat's or cow's milk

2 tablespoons coconut oil

3 cups tigernut flour

1 1/2 cups coconut sugar

3 teaspoons chia seeds

1 teaspoon baking soda

1/4 cup sunflower seeds

DIRECTIONS

1. Preheat the oven to 350°F. Line a 12-cup muffin tin with paper wrappers, or grease with coconut oil.

2. Soak the goji berries in hot water for an hour at room temperature.

3. Transfer the orange to a large bowl, add the eggs, milk, coconut oil, tigernut flour, coconut sugar, chia seeds, and baking soda, and whisk to combine. Add the sunflower seeds. Drain the goji berries and add the berries to the mixture, then mix with a spoon until well combined. Pour into the prepared muffin tin, filling each cup three-quarters full.

4. Bake for 25 to 30 minutes, or until a toothpick inserted in the center of a muffin comes out clean. Allow to cool in the pan for 10 minutes, then remove to cool completely.

+ Gluten-Free,
+ Grain-Free
+ Refined Sugar-Free
+ Soy-free
+ Vegetarian

Total time: 20 minutes
Makes: 8–10 pancakes

I have very fond memories of making pancakes with my grandma. This gluten-free version is made with a few simple ingredients and tastes fluffy and light, just like my grandmother's classic wheat-flour pancakes. My family enjoys them every weekend at home—sometimes we even have them for dinner!

FLUFFY GRAIN FREE PANCAKES

INGREDIENTS

3/4 cup cassava flour

1/3 cup coconut flour

1/2 teaspoon baking soda

1 1/2 cups goat's or cow's milk

3 large eggs, lightly beaten

1/3 cup melted ghee or butter

1 tablespoon vanilla extract

DIRECTIONS

1. In a large bowl, combine the cassava flour, coconut flour, and baking soda and stir to mix. Make a well in the center of the dry mixture and pour in the milk, eggs, ghee or butter, and vanilla extract. Slowly fold in the dry mixture from the sides until the dry and wet ingredients begin coming together, then continue to mix with a whisk until smooth.

2. Lightly grease a large frying pan and place over medium heat. Working in batches, scoop approximately 1/4 cup batter for each pancake onto the frying pan. Cook on the first side until the edges are dry and browning and the centers are bubbling, 2 to 3 minutes, then flip and cook on the second side until brown, 1 to 2 minutes. Transfer the cooked pancakes to a plate and repeat with the remaining batter.

3. Serve immediately with berries and maple syrup.

+ Gluten-Free
+ Grain-Free
+ Sugar-Free
+ Soy-free
+ Vegetarian

Total time: 20 minutes
Makes: 8–10 pancakes

This is the perfect homemade vegan pancake recipe. You have to be patient with plant-based pancakes because they're more delicate than regular pancakes—try not to flip them too early or before they set. You can purchase premade oat flour or make your own, which is a fairly simple process—just take any type of gluten-free oats and pulse them in a food processor until they resemble a flour.

OATMEAL-FLOUR PANCAKES

INGREDIENTS

1 1/2 cups tigernut flour

1/2 cup gluten-free oat flour

1/3 cup ground flaxseed

1/4 cup tapioca flour

1/4 cup arrowroot powder

1/2 teaspoon baking soda

1 1/4 cups cashew milk or almond milk

1 cup unsweetened applesauce

1/2 cup coconut oil

1 teaspoon vanilla extract

Optional: 1/2 cup dairy-free chocolate chips, sweetened with coconut sugar

DIRECTIONS

1. In a large bowl, combine the tigernut flour, oat flour, ground flaxseed, tapioca flour, arrowroot powder, and baking soda and stir to mix. Make a well in the center of the dry mixture and pour in the dairy-free milk, applesauce, coconut oil, and vanilla extract; slowly fold in the dry mixture from the sides until the dry and wet ingredients begin
coming together, then continue to mix with a whisk, spoon, or electric mixer until smooth. Fold the chocolate chips into the batter, if using, until they are evenly distributed.

2. Lightly grease a large frying pan with coconut oil and place over medium-high heat. Working in batches, scoop approximately 1/4 cup batter for each pancake onto the frying pan. Cook on the first side until the edges are dry and browning and the centers are bubbling, 2 to 3 minutes, then flip and cook on the second side until brown, 1 to 2 minutes. Transfer the cooked pancakes to a plate and repeat with the remaining batter. Serve immediately with berries, maple syrup, or honey if desired.

+ Gluten-Free
+ Sugar-Free
+ Plant-Based
+ Soy-free Option

Total time: 30 minutes
Makes 8–10 waffles

Say goodbye to tasteless frozen waffles and enjoy this flavorful homemade version instead! This grain-free waffle recipe is as easy as it is delicious—just throw all the ingredients together in one bowl and cook in your waffle iron for crispy, satisfying waffles in no time.

COCONUT-FLOUR WAFFLES

INGREDIENTS

1 1/2 cups goat's or cow's milk

3 large eggs

1/3 cup melted ghee or butter

1 teaspoon vanilla extract, optional

1/2 cup plus 2 tablespoons coconut flour

1/4 cup arrowroot powder

1/2 teaspoon baking soda

DIRECTIONS

1. Preheat a waffle iron.

2. In a large bowl, whisk together the milk, eggs, ghee, and vanilla extract, if using.

3. Add the coconut flour, arrowroot powder, and baking soda and mix well with the whisk until smooth.

4. Spray the preheated waffle iron with cooking spray. Pour 1/4 cup batter per waffle into the hot waffle iron, gently spreading just a bit before closing. Cook until golden brown, about a minute, depending on the heat in your waffle iron. Repeat with the remaining batter.

5. Serve immediately with maple syrup or honey.

+ Gluten-Free
+ Grain-Free
+ Sugar-Free
+ Soy-Free Option
+ Vegetarian

Active time: 10 minutes
Total time: 25 minutes
Makes: 12 cookies

Coconut Butter Power Seed Cookies are my favorite, and have become my signature cookies—they are soft, nutty, delicious, healthy, and extremely easy to prepare and bake. They make for a perfect on-the-go breakfast or midday snack.

COCONUT BUTTER POWER SEED COOKIES

INGREDIENTS

1 cup coconut butter, softened to room temperature

3/4 cup maple syrup

2 1/2 cups tigernut flour

1/2 cup sunflower seeds

1/2 cup pumpkin seeds

DIRECTIONS

1. Preheat the oven to 350°F. Line a large baking sheet with parchment paper and grease with coconut oil or butter.

2. In a medium bowl, cream together the coconut butter and maple syrup using a mixing spoon, or a food processor for a smoother texture. (The mixture will be super sticky). Add the tigernut flour and mix until smooth. Use a spoon or your hands to fold in the sunflower seeds and pumpkin seeds. Stir well.

3. To avoid stickiness while handling the batter, spray baking oil onto your hands. Scoop approximately 2 tablespoons of dough per cookie and use your hands to shape into individual balls. Flatten each ball and place onto the prepared baking sheet, spacing the cookies 1 to 2 inches apart.

4. Bake for 13 minutes, or until lightly browned. Let cool on the baking sheet for about 5 minutes. Transfer cookies to a cooling rack or a large plate and let cool for at least 15 more minutes before serving.

+ Gluten-Free
+ Grain-Free
+ Refined Sugar-Free
+ Soy-Free
+ Plant-Based

Active time: 10 minutes
Total time: 25 minutes
Makes: 12 large cookies

Tahini Chocolate Chip Cookies are the most requested cookies I bake, most likely because they hold the sought-after combination of being both delectable and healthy. In the past two years, I have baked hundreds of Tahini Chocolate Chip Cookies for my family, friends, and coworkers. Crispy on the outside and soft and chewy on the inside, these cookies contain nutritious tahini, which is filled with powerful antioxidants and contains healthy fats, vitamins, and minerals.

THE BEST TAHINI CHOCOLATE CHIP COOKIES

INGREDIENTS

1 cup tahini, at room temperature

1 cup maple syrup

1 tablespoon vanilla extract

1/2 teaspoon baking soda

3 cups tigernut flour

1 cup chocolate chips or chunks

DIRECTIONS

1. Preheat the oven to 350°F. Line one large or two medium baking sheets with parchment paper, then grease with coconut oil or butter.

2. In a large mixing bowl, combine the tahini, maple syrup, vanilla, and baking soda. Stir with a large spoon until the mixture is smooth. Add the tigernut flour and mix thoroughly. If your tahini butter is cold or thick, this step may take more effort. Add the chocolate chips, folding them evenly into the batter with a spoon.

3. Use a tablespoon to make even-sized cookies, or form the cookies by hand: Spray baking oil onto your hands, then take tablespoon-sized amounts of dough, shape them into balls, and flatten with your palms. Place the cookies onto the prepared baking sheet(s), leaving 1 to 2 inches of space between them.

4. Bake for 15 minutes, or until lightly browned. Let cool on the baking sheet for about 5 minutes. Transfer cookies to a cooling rack or a room-temperature plate, and let cool for at least 10 minutes more before serving.

+ Gluten-Free
+ Grain-Free
+ Refined Sugar-Free
+ Soy-Free (Option)
+ Plant-Based

Active time: 25 minutes
Total time: 1 hour 50 min
Makes: 4–5 bagels

GRAIN-FREE BAGELS

INGREDIENTS

1 1/2 teaspoons active dry yeast

1/2 teaspoon coconut sugar

3/4 cup warm water

1 1/2 tablespoons ground chia seeds

1 1/2 tablespoons ground flaxseed

1 tablespoon tigernut or olive oil

2 teaspoons apple cider vinegar

2 cups tigernut flour

1/3 cup arrowroot powder

1/3 cup tapioca flour

1/2 teaspoon baking soda

1/2 teaspoon baking powder, aluminum free

1/2 teaspoon salt

2 tablespoons poppy seeds

2 tablespoons sesame seeds

+ Gluten-Free
+ Grain-Free
+ Refined Sugar-Free
+ Soy-Free
+ Plant-Based

DIRECTIONS

1. Combine the yeast and coconut sugar with the warm water and let sit for about 10 minutes to allow the yeast to activate. Add the chia seeds, flaxseed, oil, and vinegar and let sit for 5 minutes more to allow the chia and flax to thicken.

2. In a large bowl, whisk together the tigernut flour, arrowroot flour, tapioca flour, baking soda, baking powder, and salt. Add the yeast mixture to the flour mixture and stir with a wooden spoon until well combined.

3. Line a baking sheet with a piece of parchment paper and lightly dust with tigernut flour. Divide the dough into 4 or 5 even-sized balls and smooth with your hands. Dust your hands with tigernut flour, form each ball into a bagel shape, and create a hole in the middle of each one using your thumb. Cover with a clean dish towel, set in a warm place, and allow to rise for 45 minutes.

4. Preheat the oven to 375°F. One at a time, brush each of the bagels with warm water using a pastry brush or your fingers, then sprinkle the poppy seeds and sesame seeds over the top.

5. Bake for 23 to 25 minutes. The bagels are cooked when lightly brown. Transfer to a cooling rack to cool completely. When ready to eat, slice in half and toast, if desired.

Active time: 5 minutes
Total time: 10 minutes
Makes: 12oz or 1 1/3 cups

This chocolatey, creamy butter is made with real, healthy ingredients, and can be enjoyed at any time of day. I like to have it as a snack with toasted bread, or to add a little extra pizazz to my pancakes in the morning.

CHOCOLATE CREAMY BUTTER

INGREDIENTS

1/2 cup coconut oil

1 cup tigernut flour, sifted

1 tablespoon cacao powder

3 tablespoons maple syrup

1 teaspoon vanilla extract

DIRECTIONS

1. Melt the coconut oil in a saucepan over very low heat.

2. Transfer the melted coconut oil to a food processor and add the tigernut flour, cacao powder, maple syrup, and vanilla extract. Process, stopping to scrape down the sides with a spatula every now and then, until creamy and smooth, about 1 minute.

3. Once the chocolate butter has reached your desired consistency, transfer it to a glass jar and store in the fridge for up to a month. It will harden up when it gets cold, so take it out of the fridge a few hours before serving. Serve at room temperature with toast or pancakes.

+ Gluten-Free
+ Grain-Free
+ Refined Sugar-Free
+ Soy-Free
+ Plant-Based

Active time: 10 minutes
Total time: 25 minutes
Makes: 12 cookies

Breakfast is said to be the most important meal of the day, and for good reason: It provides our body with the foundation it needs to keep us going and feeling good for the rest of the day, so it is of utmost importance that we ingest a wholesome meal containing all the nutrients our body needs. These cookies do just that—they are loaded with oats and, like all my baked goods, completely free of refined sugar. This makes them a great way to start your day on a healthy note, without sacrificing even an ounce of tastiness.

Enjoy these Peanut Butter Breakfast Cookies for breakfast or as a savory snack throughout the day. If you have a peanut allergy or are just looking for a new taste, these can also be made with almond butter.

PEANUT BUTTER BREAKFAST COOKIES

INGREDIENTS

1 cup maple syrup

1 cup peanut butter

1/2 teaspoon baking soda

2 cups tigernut flour

1 cup gluten-free quick-cooking oats

3/4 cup dried cranberries

DIRECTIONS

1. Preheat the oven to 350°F. Line a large baking sheet with parchment paper, or grease with vegan butter and lightly dust with tigernut flour.

2. In a large mixing bowl, combine the maple syrup, peanut butter, and baking soda and mix with a spoon or electric mixer until well combined. Add the tigernut flour and mix until smooth (how long this will take will depend on the temperature and consistency of your peanut butter). Fold in the oats and cranberries with a spoon until they are evenly dispersed.

3. Use a cookie scoop or a spoon to drop heaping tablespoonfuls of dough onto the prepared baking sheet, or form tablespoon-sized balls of dough with your hands and place on the baking sheet, spacing them 2 inches apart.

4. Bake for 16 to 18 minutes, or until lightly browned. Let cool on the baking sheet for about 5 minutes. Transfer cookies to a cooling rack or a room-temperature plate and let cool for 10 more minutes before serving.

+ Gluten-Free
+ Refined Sugar-Free
+ Soy-Free
+ Plant-Based

Active time: 10 minutes
Total time: 30 minutes
Makes: 9 cups

This nutritious granola is sweetened with maple syrup instead of sugar. I have always loved chocolate in my cereal, and this recipe is the perfect way for any chocolate lover to start the day; it also makes a great midday snack. Enjoy with milk, sprinkled over yogurt, or by itself.

CRUNCHY GRAIN FREE CHOCOLATE GRANOLA WITH COCONUT FLAKES

INGREDIENTS

4 cups sliced tigernuts

4 cups coconut flakes, divided

1/2 cup cacao powder

1/2 cup sunflower seeds

1/2 cup pumpkin seeds

1 cup maple syrup

1/4 cup coconut oil

1 tablespoon vanilla extract

DIRECTIONS

1. Preheat the oven to 350°F.

2. In a large bowl, combine the tigernuts, 3 cups of the coconut flakes, the cacao powder, sunflower seeds, and pumpkin seeds and stir to mix well.

3. Slowly add the maple syrup, coconut oil, and vanilla extract and mix with a spoon until well combined.

4. Pour the granola onto a baking sheet and spread into an even layer with your hands or a spatula. Bake for 20 to 25 minutes, until deep golden brown. If it is hard enough to clink when you tap it with a spoon.

5. Sprinkle the remaining cup of coconut flakes over the baked granola and let cool on the baking sheet for about 2 hours, or until completely cooled, then gently stir and scoop into a serving or storage container. Serve immediately or store in an airtight container at room temperature for up to 1 month.

+ Gluten-Free
+ Grain-Free
+ Refined Sugar-Free
+ Soy-Free
+ Plant-Based

+ SMOOTHIES, JUICES AND DRINKS

Active time: 5 minutes
Total time: 24 hours
Makes: 4 cups

All you need to make this fresh, creamy drink is raw tigernuts, water, and a blender. Tigernuts are nutrient-dense and have many health benefits. They are also known as chufa or earth almonds. Despite the name, they are not actually nuts, they are root vegetables—edible tubers. They are a rich source of antioxidants that may help improve your immune system, and are high in insoluble fiber, which may help improve your digestion.

The longer you soak the tigernuts, the creamier the milk will be. The milk is naturally more sweet than any other dairy-free milk, even without sweetener.

TIGERNUT MILK

INGREDIENTS

1 cup raw tigernuts

4 cups water

4 to 6 pitted dates and/or 2 tablespoons raw honey or maple syrup, optional, to sweeten

DIRECTIONS

1. Wash the tigernuts well, then combine them with the water and soak for 24 to 48 hours in the fridge. Transfer the tigernuts and their soaking liquid to a high-speed blender, add the dates, honey, or maple syrup, if using, and blend until smooth and frothy, 2 to 3 minutes. Strain the milk through cheesecloth to remove any remaining impurities.
Serve immediately, or store for 4 to 5 days in the refrigerator.

Tips:
1. After straining the milk, reserve any leftover tigernut pulp. Spread the pulp out on a baking sheet and bake at 200°F for 3 hours to dry it out. The dried pulp can be used in homemade granola or cookie recipes or added to smoothies.

2. The milk can be frozen in ice cube trays and stored in the freezer for up to 4 months. Use the frozen cubes to add thickness to smoothies and shakes instead of relying on bananas or other super-sweet frozen fruit—this will dramatically lessen the sugar content of your smoothies.

+ Gluten-Free
+ Grain-Free
+ Refined Sugar-Free
+ Soy-Free
+ Plant-Based
+ Raw/No-Bake

This homemade chocolate milk is rich and indulgent despite being dairy-free, and more delicious than any store-bought brand.

DAIRY-FREE CHOCOLATE MILK

INGREDIENTS

3 cups Tigernut Milk (page 62) or any dairy-free milk

1/4 cup plus 1 tablespoon maple syrup

1 tablespoon vanilla extract

2 tablespoons cacao powder

DIRECTIONS

1. Combine the tigernut milk, maple syrup, vanilla extract, and cacao powder in a blender and blend for 1 minute, or until smooth.

2. Serve immediately or store in the refrigerator for up to 4 days in a sealed container. Serve chilled.

+ Gluten-Free
+ Grain-Free
+ Refined Sugar-Free
+ Soy-Free
+ Dairy-Free
+ Raw/No-Bake

Total time: 5 minutes
Serves: 2–4

This iced latte is out-of-this-world delicious. I love serving it in a fancy glass jar with a straw. I like to use cold-brew coffee to make it, because it tastes better and is less acidic.

ICED COFFEE LATTE

INGREDIENTS

4 cups Tigernut Milk (page 62)

3/4 cup cold-brew coffee, home-made (page 66) or store-bought

1/4 cup maple syrup

DIRECTIONS

1. Combine the tigernut milk, cold-brew coffee, and maple syrup in a pitcher and whisk until well combined. Serve over ice and enjoy.

+ Gluten-Free
+ Grain-Free
+ Refined Sugar-Free
+ Soy-Free, Plant-Based
+ Raw/No-Bake

Active time: 5 minutes
Total time: 12 hours
Makes: 4 cups

HOMEMADE COLD-BREW COFFEE

INGREDIENTS

1 cup ground coffee
4 cups filtered water

DIRECTIONS

1. Combine the coffee and filtered water in a glass jar, stir well, and refrigerate overnight.

2. Strain the coffee through a piece of cheesecloth into another clean glass jar. Serve immediately over ice, or cover and refrigerate for up to 2 weeks.

+ Gluten-Free
+ Grain-Free
+ Sugar-Free
+ Plant-Based
+ Soy-Free
+ Raw/No-Bake

This is a creamy, delicious, cold matcha latte that everyone can enjoy. Matcha is another superfood that is packed with antioxidants. It may boost metabolism and burn calories, and it naturally detoxifies the body. Rich with chlorophyll and vitamins, it might even improve your mood and concentration. I love using ceremonial-grade matcha rather than culinary grade because it is more flavorful. For extra flavor you can add vanilla extract.

ICED MATCHA LATTE

INGREDIENTS

1 teaspoon matcha green tea powder

1/4 cup hot water

1 cup unsweetened Tigernut Milk (page 62) or almond milk

2 tablespoons maple syrup, or more to taste

1 teaspoon vanilla extract, optional

DIRECTIONS

1. In a large jar, combine the matcha powder and hot water and stir to form a smooth paste with no clumps.

2. Pour the tigernut milk over the matcha tea, add the maple syrup and vanilla extract, if using, and stir until well combined. Let sit for a minute so any remaining clumps settle to the bottom. Pour into a glass over ice and enjoy cold.

+ Gluten-Free
+ Grain-Free
+ Refined Sugar-Free
+ Plant-Based
+ Soy-Free
+ Raw/No-Bake

Total time: 5 minutes
Serves: 4

Turmeric, a spice that is also used in curry, adds a unique and exotic flavor to this rich, comforting drink. Turmeric is a powerful anti-inflammatory and antioxidant. It is better absorbed into the bloodstream if used with black pepper, which enhances its absorption.

ICED GOLDEN MILK LATTE

INGREDIENTS

4 cups cold Tigernut Milk (page 62) or almond milk

1/4 cup cold-pressed turmeric juice OR 1 1/2 teaspoons ground turmeric

3 tablespoons maple syrup or honey, or more to taste

1 tablespoon coconut oil, optional

1 teaspoon ground cinnamon

1/2 teaspoon ground black pepper

DIRECTIONS

1. In a high-speed blender, combine the tigernut or almond milk, turmeric, maple syrup or honey, coconut oil, if using, cinnamon, and black pepper. Blend until smooth and frothy. Serve immediately over ice, or store in the refrigerator for up to 5 days.

+ Gluten-Free
+ Grain-free
+ Refined Sugar-Free
+ Plant-Based
+ Soy-Free
+ Raw/No-Bake

Total time: 5 minutes
Serves 2

Horchata is a plant-based drink that originated in Valencia, Spain, and is traditionally made with tigernuts. Horchata is also very popular in Mexico and Central America, where it is usually made with rice milk. This rich and creamy grain-free version is made from tigernuts instead of rice, and is sweetened with date syrup, maple syrup, or honey.

HORCHATA

INGREDIENTS

4 cups cold Tigernut Milk (page 62)

2 tablespoons maple syrup or honey, or more to taste

1 teaspoon vanilla extract

1 tablespoon ground cinnamon

1/2 teaspoon ground cloves

1/2 teaspoon ground nutmeg

DIRECTIONS

1. Combine all the ingredients in a high-speed blender and blend until smooth and frothy. Serve immediately over ice, or store for up to 5 days in the refrigerator.

+ Gluten-Free
+ Refined Sugar-Free
+ Soy-Free
+ Plant-Based
+ Raw/No-Bake

CHOCOLATE-BANANA SMOOTHIE

INGREDIENTS

1 cup cold Tigernut Milk (page 62) or any dairy-free milk

1 banana, peeled

1/3 cup peanut butter (or any other nut or seed butter)

2 tablespoons cacao powder

DIRECTIONS

1. Combine all the ingredients in a blender or food processor and pulse until well blended. Serve immediately.

+ Gluten-Free
+ Grain-Free
+ Sugar-Free
+ Soy-Free
+ Plant-Based
+ Raw/no-bake

Total time: 5 minutes
Serves: 2

This simple protein smoothie is creamy and packed with nutrients. While it is already a bit sweet from the naturally-occurring sugar in the fruit, you can add maple syrup as an extra sweetener if desired.

SUPER PROTEIN SMOOTHIE

INGREDIENTS

1 cup cold water or dairy-free milk

1 cup frozen blueberries

2 tablespoons cashew butter (or any other nut or seed butter)

2 tablespoons whey protein powder

1 tablespoon chia seeds

1 tablespoon maple syrup, optional

DIRECTIONS

1. Combine the water or milk, blueberries, cashew butter, whey protein, chia seeds, and maple syrup, if using, in a blender or food processor and pulse until well blended. Add the ice, if using, and blend again until smooth. Divide the smoothie between two glasses and serve immediately.

+ Gluten-Free
+ Grain-Free
+ Refined Sugar-Free
+ Soy-Free
+ Vegetarian
+ Raw/No- Bake

This berry smoothie is easy to make and tastes great. Its fruity flavor is very refreshing, which makes it my go-to for a quick breakfast or snack.

EASY BLUEBERRY SMOOTHIE

INGREDIENTS

1 cup cold Tigernut Milk (page 62) or almond milk

3/4 cup frozen blueberries

4 or 5 frozen strawberries (about 1/2 cup)

1/4 cup frozen spinach

2 medjool dates, pitted

1 tablespoon almond butter

DIRECTIONS

1. Combine all the ingredients in a blender or food processor and blend until smooth. Serve immediately.

+ Gluten-Free
+ Grain-Free
+ Refined Sugar-Free
+ Soy-Free
+ Plant-Based
+ Raw/No-Bake

This smoothie's bright pink color and sweet flavor are very appealing for kids and adults alike. It is jam-packed with nutrients and can be prepared in just five minutes.

STRAWBERRY-LEMON ZEST SMOOTHIE

INGREDIENTS

1 cup cold Tigernut Milk (page 62) or any dairy-free milk

16 frozen strawberries

1 banana, peeled

2 tablespoons whey protein powder

1 tablespoon maple syrup, optional

1 teaspoon lemon zest

DIRECTIONS

1. Combine all the ingredients in a high-speed blender and blend until smooth. Serve immediately.

+ Gluten-Free
+ Grain-Free
+ Refined Sugar-Free
+ Soy-Free
+ Vegetarian

Total time: 5 minutes
Serves: 2

This is one of the healthiest and most delectable smoothies I make—and I have been making smoothies for a very long time! I love sharing my favorite smoothies with guests when they come over as a change of pace from the traditional coffee or tea.

AVOCADO, BANANA & DATE SMOOTHIE

INGREDIENTS

1 3/4 cups Tigernut Milk (page 62) or almond milk

1 avocado, peeled and pit removed

1 ripe peeled banana, fresh or frozen

3 Medjool dates, pitted

1 handful of frozen spinach

A few ice cubes

DIRECTIONS

1. Combine the tigernut or almond milk, avocado, banana, dates, and spinach in a high-speed blender and blend until smooth. Add the ice cubes and blend again. Divide the smoothie between two glasses and serve immediately.

+ Gluten-Free
+ Grain-Free
+ Refined Sugar-Free
+ Soy-Free
+ Plant-Based
+ Raw/No-Bake

Total time: 5 minutes
Serves: 1

I drink this smoothie as a supplement to my breakfast or afternoon snack. It contains only four ingredients plus ice, and is super easy to make.

KALE-BANANA SMOOTHIE

INGREDIENTS

1 cup cold water or dairy-free milk

1 cup frozen chopped kale

1 peeled banana, fresh or frozen

3 Medjool dates, pitted

A few ice cubes, optional

DIRECTIONS

1. Combine the water or milk, kale, banana, and dates in a blender or food processor and pulse until well combined. Add the ice cubes, if using, and blend until smooth. Pour the smoothie into a glass and serve immediately.

+ Gluten-Free
+ Grain-Free
+ Refined Sugar-Free
+ Soy-Free
+ Plant-Based,
+ Raw/No-Bake

Total time: 5 minutes
Serves: 1

When I'm craving a dessert, I often make this milkshake. It tastes as good as a traditional milkshake, but is much healthier and more flavorful. I frequently serve this to my guests and watch as it wins them over.

QUICK BANANA MILKSHAKE

INGREDIENTS

1 large ripe banana, peeled, cut into chunks, and frozen overnight

2 cups cold Tigernut Milk (page 62) or almond milk

2 tablespoons maple syrup

1 tablespoon almond butter

1/2 teaspoon ground cinnamon

Pinch of ground cardamom

DIRECTIONS

1. Combine all the ingredients in a high-speed blender and blend until smooth.

2. Pour the milkshake into a glass and serve immediately.

+ Gluten-Free
+ Grain-Free
+ Refined Sugar-Free
+ Soy-free
+ Plant-Based
+ Raw/No-Bake

Strawberry always seems to evoke childhood memories for me. When I was younger, I used to melt vanilla ice cream and then blend it with strawberries. It always made me happy, and even back then I loved sharing my recipes with my family. Who would have thought that years later, this plant-based version of that childhood recipe would become everyone's favorite?

This milkshake reminds me of how grateful I am to my family for allowing me to hone my craft and supporting me throughout it all— even when my original milkshakes were a bit of a disaster, my family always encouraged me to keep at it and never give up.

EASY STRAWBERRY MILKSHAKE

INGREDIENTS

1 cup frozen or fresh strawberries

2 cups cold Tigernut Milk (page 62) or almond milk

1/4 cup maple syrup or honey

A few ice cubes (if using fresh strawberries; omit if using frozen berries)

DIRECTIONS

1. If using fresh strawberries, hull the berries. Place the strawberries in a high speed blender or food processor, add the tigernut or almond milk and maple syrup or honey, and blend until smooth. Add the ice cubes, if using, and blend again until smooth. Divide the milkshake between two glasses and serve immediately.

+ Gluten-Free
+ Grain-Free
+ Refined Sugar-Free
+ Soy-Free
+ Plant-Based
+ Raw/No-Bake

Smoothie bowls have become a very popular meal among millennials, and they couldn't be easier to make at home—all that's required is a small bowl of your favorite smoothie topped with superfood ingredients and chopped fruit. This is a great breakfast and easy to customize—just change the toppings to enjoy a different flavor every morning.

PROTEIN SMOOTHIE BOWL

INGREDIENTS

1 large ripe avocado, peeled and pit removed

1 cup fresh or frozen strawberries

1 large handful fresh or frozen kale

1 small handful fresh or frozen spinach

5 Medjool dates, pitted

2 tablespoons almond butter

1 1/2 cups cold Tigernut Milk (page 62) or almond milk

Optional toppings:

Chia seeds

Hemp seeds

Fresh berries

Sunflower seeds

Shredded coconut

DIRECTIONS

1. Combine the avocado, strawberries, kale, spinach, dates, and almond butter in a blender or food processor and pulse until smooth. Add the tigernut milk and blend until well combined. Pour the smoothie into a bowl and sprinkle with your favorite toppings.

+ Gluten-Free
+ Grain-free
+ Refined Sugar-Free
+ Soy-Free
+ Plant-Based
+ Raw/No-Bake

+ CRACKERS AND BREADS

+ Cauliflower Pizza Dough 86

+ Sun-Dried Tomato Olive Crackers 89

+ Sea Salt Grain-Free Crackers 90

+ Rosemary Crackers 91

+ Gluten-Free Bread 93

Active time: 20 minutes
Total time: 40 minutes
Serves: 4–6

We eat a lot of cauliflower in my family, because I like to add it to pretty much any meal. This amazing pizza dough can be enjoyed as a simple vegan dish by adding just vegan toppings—or you can add any of your favorite toppings, from classic red sauce and basil to fresh tomatoes, sautéed onions, pesto, goat cheese, and more. You'll only need to use 1 cup of riced cauliflower for the dough; the leftover cauliflower rice can be kept in the fridge for a few days or frozen for up to a month.

CAULIFLOWER PIZZA DOUGH

INGREDIENTS

1 small head fresh cauliflower

2 cups tigernut flour

1/4 cup ground flaxseed

1/4 cup sorghum flour or gluten-free oat flour

2 tablespoons nutritional yeast

1 teaspoon baking powder

1 teaspoon salt

1 teaspoon dried oregano

1/2 teaspoon dried basil

1/4 teaspoon garlic powder

1 cup hot water

1/4 cup olive oil

DIRECTIONS

1. Preheat the oven to 475°F. Line a baking sheet with parchment paper.

2. Place the cauliflower in a food processor or high-powered blender and grate until riced. Dump the grated cauliflower onto a clean tea towel or paper towel and wrap, twist, and squeeze it hard, as if wringing out a towel, to remove all liquid from the cauliflower. Transfer 1 cup of the dried cauliflower to a large bowl (reserve the rest for another use). Add the tigernut flour, flaxseed, sorghum or oat flour, nutritional yeast, baking powder, salt, oregano, basil, garlic powder, water, and oil and mix by hand until well combined.

3. Form the dough into a pizza shape on the prepared baking sheet, pinching the edges to make a crust. If the dough sticks to your fingers as you spread it out, place a piece of parchment paper between your hand and the dough as you shape it.

4. Bake for about 12 minutes, or until it starts turning golden brown. Add your preferred toppings, then return to the oven and bake for another 8 to 10 minutes.

5. Slice and serve warm.

+ Gluten-Free
+ Sugar-Free
+ Soy-Free
+ Plant-Based
+ Nut-free

Active time: 10 minutes
Total time: 35 minutes
Makes: 40 crackers

These are what my son calls "magic crackers"—homemade grain-free crackers that are easy to make and rich in flavor. But it's the fact that these crackers provide a healthy alternative for my son to snack on that makes them truly magical.

SUN-DRIED TOMATO OLIVE CRACKERS

INGREDIENTS

3 flax eggs (see step 2)

2 cups tigernut flour

1 tablespoon arrowroot powder

1/4 cup warm water, plus additional as needed

2 tablespoons olive oil

1/4 cup sun-dried tomatoes, diced

1/4 cup pitted mixed olives, diced

1/2 teaspoon sea salt, plus additional for sprinkling

1/2 teaspoon dried basil, plus additional for sprinkling

1/2 teaspoon ground black pepper

+ Gluten-Free
+ Grain-Free
+ Sugar-Free
+ Soy-Free
+ Plant-Based

DIRECTIONS

1. Preheat the oven to 350°F. Line a baking sheet with parchment paper.

2. To make the flax eggs, stir together 3 tablespoons ground flaxseed and 9 tablespoons water in a small bowl, transfer to the refrigerator, and chill for at least 10 minutes.

3. In a large bowl, combine half of the flax eggs with the tigernut flour, arrowroot powder, warm water, and olive oil and mix with your hands, or mix in a food processor until well combined. Add the sun-dried tomatoes, olives, sea salt, basil, and pepper and mix with your hands. If the dough feels too hard to work with, add up to 3 tablespoons of additional water little by little until the desired consistency is reached. Form the dough into a round and place on the prepared baking sheet. Place another piece of parchment paper between your hand and the dough to prevent sticking, and use the palm of your hand to flatten the dough to about 1/8 inch thick.

4. Use a cookie cutter or knife to cut about 40 crackers in your desired shape. Whisk the remaining half of the flax egg in a small bowl, then brush it on top of each cracker. Top the crackers with extra sea salt and dried basil.

5. Bake for 15 to 20 minutes, or until browned. Let sit on the baking sheet for about 15 minutes, then transfer, being careful not to break them, to a plate or wire rack and let cool for about 45 more minutes before serving. Serve with spreadable cheese, dip, or pesto.

Active time: 10 minutes
Total time: 45 minutes
Makes: 40 crackers

It can be difficult to find grain-free crackers in the store, and when you do find them, they are never cheap. Instead, you can make them at home with this easy recipe—and besides, homemade crackers taste better anyway! These crackers are a perfect snack and very easy to make. I love to serve them with dips or cheese.

SEA SALT GRAIN-FREE CRACKERS

INGREDIENTS

2 flax eggs (see step 2)

3 tablespoons olive oil

2 1/2 cups tigernut flour

2 teaspoons salt

1/2 teaspoon black pepper

Maldon sea salt flakes, for sprinkling

DIRECTIONS

1. Preheat the oven to 350°F. Line a baking sheet with parchment paper.

2. To make the flax eggs, stir together 2 tablespoons ground flaxseed and 6 tablespoons water in a small bowl, transfer to the refrigerator, and chill for at least 15 to 20 minutes.

3. In a food processor, combine the flax eggs, oil, tigernut flour, salt, and pepper pulse into a dough, and place on the prepared baking sheet. Place another piece of parchment paper between your hand and the dough to prevent sticking, and use the palm of your hand to flatten the dough to a 1/8-inch thickness.

4. Use a cookie cutter or knife to cut about 40 crackers in your desired shape. Sprinkle the Maldon sea salt over the top.

5. Bake for about 20 minutes, or until browned. Let sit on the baking sheet for about 15 minutes, then transfer, being careful not to break them, to a plate or wire rack and let cool for about 45 more minutes before serving. Serve with spreadable cheese, dip, or pesto.

+ Gluten-Free
+ Grain-Free
+ Sugar-Free
+ Soy-Free
+ Plant-Based
+ Nut-Free

Active time: 10 minutes
Total time: 45 minutes
Makes: 20 crackers

ROSEMARY CRACKERS

INGREDIENTS

3 chia seed eggs (see step 2)

1/4 cup olive oil

1/2 cup tigernut flour

1/4 cup sun-dried tomatoes, diced small

1/4 cup hemp seeds

Pinch of dried rosemary

Pinch of garlic powder

Pinch of salt

1 teaspoon dried basil, for sprinkling

Pinch of sea salt, for sprinkling

DIRECTIONS

1. Preheat the oven to 350°F. Line a baking sheet with parchment paper.

2. To make the chia seed eggs, combine 1/4 cup ground chia seeds and 3/4 cup hot water in a small bowl, transfer to the refrigerator, and chill for at least 10 minutes.

3. In a large bowl, combine the chia seed eggs, oil, tigernut flour, sun-dried tomatoes, hemp seeds, rosemary, garlic powder, and salt and mix with your hands. Gather the dough and place on the prepared baking sheet. Place another piece of parchment paper between your hand and the dough to prevent sticking, then use the palm of your hand to flatten the dough to a 1/8-inch thickness.

4. Use a cookie cutter or knife to cut about 20 crackers in your desired shape. Sprinkle the dried basil and sea salt over the top.

5. Bake for 20 to 25 minutes, or until browned. Let sit on the baking sheet for about 15 minutes, then transfer, being careful not to break them, to a plate or wire rack and let cool completely, about 45 more minutes, before serving. Serve with spreadable cheese, Tigernut Butter Spread (page 104), or pesto.

+ Gluten-Free
+ Grain-Free
+ Sugar-Free
+ Soy-Free
+ Plant-Based
+ Nut-Free

Active time: 10 minutes
Total time: 3 hours 55 min
Makes: 1x 8 1/2" x 4 1/2" loaf

I have a friend who has celiac disease and had to change her entire lifestyle when she found out. Although the selection of gluten-free items in stores has gotten better in recent years, she has always had a hard time finding a truly good-quality gluten-free bread to buy, so I created this recipe for her. Besides, nothing is better than homemade bread!

GLUTEN-FREE BREAD

INGREDIENTS

7 grams active dry yeast

1 1/2 teaspoons salt

2 1/4 cups warm water

3 cups buckwheat flour

3/4 cup tigernut flour

1/4 cup sunflour seeds

DIRECTIONS

1. Combine the yeast and salt, then add the water, mix well, and let sit for 15 minutes to allow the yeast to activate.

2. Combine the buckwheat and tigernut flours in a bowl and create a well in the center. Pour the yeast/water mixture into the well, then stir well with a spoon until you have a thick batter that drops sluggishly off the spoon. Cover with a kitchen towel and put in a warm place to rise for about 2 hours.

3. Once the mixture has risen, preheat the oven to 350°F and lightly grease an 8 1/2-x-4 1/2-inch loaf pan. Pour the batter into the prepared pan, spread it out evenly and sprinkle with the sunflower seeds on the top. Bake for 60 minutes, until brown and firm to the touch, or until the inside temperature is about 200°F. Let the loaf sit and rest before removing from the pan, about 30 minutes, then slice and serve.

+ Gluten-Free
+ Sugar-Free
+ Soy-Free
+ Plant-Based
+ Nut-Free

Active time: 10 minutes
Total time: 15 minutes
Serves: 4–6

Spreads are always on my menu during holiday parties and family gatherings. This recipe makes for a great appetizer to snack on while socializing with your friends and family, and the beauty is that unlike most party foods, it is also healthy!

SPINACH DIP

INGREDIENTS

2 pounds spinach

1 1/4 cups chopped walnuts

1/2 bunch cilantro, leaves and stems

1/2 bunch parsley, leaves and stems

1 garlic clove, peeled

1/4 cup olive oil

1–2 tablespoons apple cider vinegar, or more to taste

1/2 teaspoon sea salt, or more to taste

DIRECTIONS

1. Bring a pot of water to a boil. Add the washed spinach and boil for 2 to 3 minutes, until softened. Drain the spinach in a colander, rinse with cold water to stop the cooking, and squeeze out as much liquid from it as you can by squeezing one handful at a time between your hands. Set aside.

2. Place the walnuts in a food processor or blender and pulse until coarsely chopped. Add the spinach, cilantro, parsley, garlic, oil, vinegar, and salt and pulse until the mixture reaches a slightly chunky consistency. If it is too thick, add 1 to 2 tablespoons water and pulse again. Taste and add more vinegar and/or salt as needed.

3. Serve at room temperature with Gluten-Free Bread (page 93) or Sea Salt Grain-Free Crackers (page 90).

+ Gluten-Free
+ Grain-Free
+ Sugar-Free
+ Soy-Free
+ Plant-Based

Active time: 10 minutes
Total time: 40 minutes
Serves: 4

BEET SPREAD

INGREDIENTS

4 medium-size beets, greens removed

1/2 cup tigernut flour or 1 cup chopped walnuts

1/3 cup chopped cilantro

1/4 cup olive oil

1–2 tablespoons apple cider vinegar, or more to taste

1/2 teaspoon salt

1 garlic clove, optional

1 tablespoon fresh dill, chopped, for garnish

DIRECTIONS

1. Place the beets in a large pot and fill with water to cover. Bring to a boil over medium heat. Lower the heat to medium-low and cook until the beets are fork-tender, about 30 minutes.

2. Remove from the heat, drain the beets, and let cool. Once the beets are cool enough to handle, peel and cut each one into quarters.

3. Transfer the beets to a food processor and add the tigernut flour or walnuts, cilantro, olive oil, vinegar, salt, and garlic, if using. Blend until coarsely chopped.

4. Transfer the dip to a serving bowl, garnish with the chopped dill, and serve with bread or crackers.

+ Gluten-Free
+ Grain-Free
+ Sugar-Free
+ Soy-Free
+ Plant-Based

Active time: 10 minutes
Total time: 25 minutes
Serves: 4

My family loves homemade dips and spreads, and this is one of our favorites to serve with fresh veggies or crackers.

SPICY CARROT SPREAD

INGREDIENTS

6 medium carrots

1/2 cup tahini

1/4 cup olive oil

1–2 garlic cloves

2 teaspoons curry powder

1 teaspoon sea salt

1/2 teaspoon chile pepper flakes

DIRECTIONS

1. Place the carrots in a large pot, fill with water to cover, and bring to a boil over medium heat. Lower the heat to medium-low and cook until the carrots are fork-tender, about 13 minutes.

2. Remove from the heat, drain the carrots, and let cool. Once your carrots are cool enough to handle, peel and chop each one into small cubes.

3. Transfer the carrots to a food processor and add the tahini, oil, garlic, curry powder, sea salt, and chile pepper flakes. Blend until smooth.

4. Transfer to a serving bowl and serve as a dip with crackers.

+ Gluten-Free
+ Grain-Free
+ Sugar-Free
+ Soy-Free
+ Plant-Based
+ Nut-Free

Total time: 10 minutes
Serves: 4

I love nothing more than making my own hummus. Homemade recipes are always fresher and better-tasting than store-bought versions. This delicious hummus is creamy and has an amazingly rich flavor. I call for canned chickpeas below for convenience, but you can also cook your own dried chickpeas for this recipe if you prefer.

EASY HUMMUS

INGREDIENTS

1/3 cup tahini

Juice of 1 large lemon (about 1/4 cup)

3 tablespoons olive oil, plus more for garnishing

1/2 garlic clove, minced

1 teaspoon sea salt

1/2 teaspoon cumin

1 (15-ounce) can chickpeas, drained

Small pinch of ground paprika, for garnishing

Chopped fresh parsley, for garnishing

DIRECTIONS

1. Combine the tahini, lemon juice, oil, garlic, salt, and cumin in a food processor and pulse until fluffy and smooth.

2. Add the chickpeas and process until smooth, about 2 minutes. If the hummus seems too thick, add 2 to 3 tablespoons of water a little at a time with the food processor running to thin it.

3. Transfer to a serving bowl, drizzle with olive oil, and sprinkle with the chopped parsley and a pinch of paprika before serving.

+ Gluten-Free
+ Grain-Free
+ Refined Sugar-Free
+ Soy-Free
+ Plant-Based
+ Nut-Free

Total time: 10 minutes
Serves: 4

This dressing works well on top of grilled vegetables and with a variety of salads.

CREAMY LENTIL DRESSING

INGREDIENTS

1/2 cup boiled brown or green lentils

1/2 cup dairy-free milk

1/3 cup tahini

1/4 cup olive oil

2 garlic cloves

Sea salt and pepper to taste

DIRECTIONS

1. Combine all the ingredients in a food processor and blend until thoroughly combined. Use immediately or keep in the fridge, covered, for up to 1 week. It might thicken with time; simply thin it with a little warm water before serving and enjoy.

+ Gluten-Free
+ Sugar-Free
+ Soy-Free
+ Nut-Free
+ Plant-Based

Active time: 5 minutes
Total time: 10 minutes
Makes: 12 ounces

This is a perfect recipe for nut-butter lovers—even though it contains no nuts! Tigernut is actually a root with a nutty flavor, and is filled with nutrients.

TIGERNUT BUTTER SPREAD

INGREDIENTS

1/3 cup coconut oil

1 cup tigernut flour, sifted

1 tablespoon vanilla extract

Pinch of sea salt

DIRECTIONS

1. Melt the coconut in a saucepan over very low heat.

2. Combine the melted oil, tigernut flour, vanilla extract, and salt in a food processor and blend for about 5 minutes, stopping to scrape down the sides with a spatula every now and then.

3. Once the butter is totally creamy and smooth, transfer it to a glass jar and store in the fridge for up to a month. The tigernut butter will harden when it gets cold, so remove from the fridge about an hour before serving. Serve at room temperature with toast or pancakes.

+ Gluten-Free
+ Grain-Free
+ Sugar-Free
+ Soy-Free
+ Plant-Based
+ Nut-Free

CREAMY TAHINI DRESSING

INGREDIENTS

1/3 cup tahini

1/4 cup olive oil

1/4 cup lemon juice

1/4 cup water, or more as needed

1 teaspoon turmeric

1/2 teaspoon black pepper

Pinch of salt

DIRECTIONS

1. Combine all the ingredients in a food processor or blender and pulse until well blended. If the dressing seems too thick, add up to 2 tablespoons more water as needed to thin. Use immediately, or cover and keep in the fridge for about 1 week. It might thicken with time; simply thin it with a little warm water before serving and enjoy.

+ Gluten-Free
+ Grain-Free
+ Sugar-Free
+ Soy-Free
+ Plant-Based
+ Nut-Free

Active time: 10 minutes
Total time: 30 minutes
Serves: 4–6

My eggplant stew is creamy, full of flavor, and super simple to make. Even non-eggplant lovers will enjoy this quick, easy dish for any occasion. I prefer to peel the tomatoes for this stew, but you can skip this step if you prefer and it will still taste great. It makes a great main dish or can be used as a side with pretty much any protein.

ONE-POT EGGPLANT STEW

INGREDIENTS

2 large tomatoes (any variety)

1/3 cup olive oil

1 large eggplant, diced

2 medium potatoes, peeled and cubed

1 onion, chopped

2 garlic cloves, minced

1/4 teaspoon oregano

1/2 bunch parsley, chopped

DIRECTIONS

1. Remove the stems from the tomatoes with a paring knife. Place the tomatoes in a heatproof bowl, then fill the bowl with boiling water and soak the tomatoes for 2 to 3 minutes. Rinse with cold water and peel the skin off with a knife. Chop the tomatoes.

2. Heat the oil in a large sauté pan over medium-low heat and add the tomatoes, eggplant, potatoes, onion, garlic, and oregano. Cook, covered, for 20 minutes.

3. Remove from the heat, stir in the chopped parsley, and serve.

+ Gluten-Free
+ Grain-Free
+ Sugar-Free
+ Soy-Free
+ Plant-Based
+ Nut-Free

Active time: 10 minutes
Total time: 15 minutes
Serves: 4–6

This soup comes together in the blender or food processor in just a few minutes!

CHILLED TOMATO-AVOCADO SOUP

INGREDIENTS

2 medium tomatoes

1 avocado, peeled, pitted, and cut into chunks

2 tablespoons olive oil

1/4 teaspoon salt, or more to taste

Ground black pepper, to taste

DIRECTIONS

1. Remove the stems from the tomatoes with a paring knife. Place the tomatoes in a heatproof bowl, fill the bowl with boiling water, and soak the tomatoes for 2 to 3 minutes. Drain the tomatoes, rinse with cold water, and peel the skin off with a knife.

2. Chop the tomatoes and transfer to a food processor or blender. Add the avocado, olive oil, and salt and pulse until smooth and creamy. Season with black pepper and more salt, if needed, before serving. Serve immediately with gluten-free bread or crackers.

+ Gluten-Free
+ Grain-Free
+ Sugar-Free
+ Soy-Free
+ Plant-Based
+ Nut-Free
+ Raw/No-Bake

Active time: 5 minutes
Total time: 5 minutes
Serves: 1

EASY RAW PARSLEY-AVOCODO SOUP

INGREDIENTS

1 avocado, peeled, pitted, and cut into chunks

1/2 bunch parsley, stems and leaves, washed

1 cup cold water

2 tablespoons olive oil

2 tablespoons lemon juice (from about 1/2 lemon)

1/4 teaspoon salt

DIRECTIONS

1. Combine all the ingredients in a food processor or high-speed blender and pulse until creamy and smooth. Serve immediately or chill to the desired temperature. This soup tastes great both cold and at room temperature.

+ Gluten-Free
+ Grain-Free
+ Sugar-Free
+ Soy-Free
+ Plant-Based
+ Nut-free
+ Raw/No-Bake

Active time: 5 minutes
Total time: 20 minutes
Serves: 4–6

This nourishing turmeric soup is made with warming spices that make it perfect during cold-weather days. Its flavor is earthy, slightly bitter, and gingery. Turmeric contains powerful antioxidants and it is immunity boosting. It holds exceptional anti-inflammatory properties, and is thought to be more effective when combined with black pepper.

IMMUNITY-BOOSTING TURMERIC VEGETABLE SOUP

INGREDIENTS

1/4 cup olive oil

1 small onion, chopped

1 cup chopped celery (about 3 stalks)

2 garlic cloves, minced

2 teaspoons grated fresh ginger

8 cups vegetable broth or water

3 cups fresh or frozen mixed assortment of vegetables, chopped (carrots, peas, corn, green beans)

1/2 cup white rice

1 1/2 tablespoons ground turmeric

1 teaspoon ground black pepper

1 teaspoon salt

1 cup chopped parsley

DIRECTIONS

1. Heat the oil in a large pot over medium heat. Add the onion, celery, garlic, and ginger and cook, stirring, for about 2 minutes.

2. Add the broth, mixed vegetables, rice, turmeric, black pepper, and salt and bring to a boil. Lower the heat and simmer covered, for about 15 minutes.

3. Remove from the heat and stir in the chopped parsley before serving.

+ Gluten-Free
+ Sugar-Free
+ Soy-Free
+ Plant-Based
+ Nut-Free

Active time: 20 minutes
Total time: 40 minutes
Serves: 4

This soup pairs perfectly with toasted buckwheat bread drizzled with olive oil. It has a delightful flavor and a creamy texture and color.

TOMATO-COCONUT SOUP

INGREDIENTS

4 large tomatoes

1/4 cup olive oil

1 medium onion, chopped

2 garlic cloves, chopped

1 medium carrot, chopped

2 cups vegetable broth or water

1/3 cup coconut milk

1/2 teaspoon salt, or more to taste

1/2 teaspoon ground black pepper, or more to taste

1/4 teaspoon cayenne pepper

1/2 teaspoon dried oregano, for garnishing

1/4 cup goat cheese crumbles, for garnishing

DIRECTIONS

1. Remove the stems from the tomatoes with a paring knife. Place the tomatoes in a heatproof bowl, fill the bowl with boiling water, and soak the tomatoes for 2 to 3 minutes. Drain the tomatoes, rinse with cold water, and peel the skin off with a knife. Dice the tomatoes and set aside.

2. Heat the oil in a medium pot over medium-low heat. Add the onion and garlic and cook, stirring, for about 5 minutes. Add the tomatoes and carrot and cook, stirring, for another 10 minutes. Add the vegetable broth or water and coconut milk and stir to combine. Increase the heat to medium-high and bring the mixture to a simmer. Cook for 20 minutes.

3. Remove the pot from the heat and let the soup cool for a few minutes, then add the salt, black pepper, and cayenne pepper. Working in batches if necessary, transfer the mixture to a blender, securely fasten the lid, and blend the soup until smooth.

4. Garnish with oregano. Serve each bowl with 1 or 2 tablespoons of goat cheese crumbles and with gluten-free crackers or bread.

+ Gluten-Free
+ Grain-Free
+ Sugar-Free
+ Soy-Free
+ Vegetarian

RAW BROCCOLI SOUP

INGREDIENTS

1 cup chopped raw broccoli

1/2 cup chopped cucumber

1/3 cup parsley leaves

1/2 teaspoon salt

Juice of 1 lemon

1 cup cold water

DIRECTIONS

1. Combine all the ingredients in a food processor or blender and pulse until well blended. Serve immediately with crackers or toast, or chill to the desired temperature and serve later.

+ Gluten-Free
+ Grain-Free
+ Sugar-Free
+ Soy-Free
+ Plant-Based
+ Nut-Free

Active time: 10 minutes
Total time: 30 minutes
Serves: 4–6

This colorful, vibrant one-pot soup makes an easy weeknight meal. The traditional Eastern European version is made with beef; however, this plant-based version is a great option for vegetarians and is just as delicious as borscht made with beef. My family enjoys both vegetarian and beef borscht equally. For the meat-lovers' version, see page 154.

RED BEET SOUP "BORSCHT"

INGREDIENTS

2 large tomatoes

1/3 cup olive oil

1 onion, chopped

1–3 garlic cloves, chopped

5 cups vegetable broth or water

2 cups chopped cabbage

1 small beet, peeled and chopped

1 large carrot, peeled and chopped

1 cup chopped potatoes (any variety)

2 bay leaves

1/4 cup chopped parsley

1/2 teaspoon salt, or more to taste

1/2 teaspoon ground black pepper, or more to taste

1/4 cup chopped fresh dill, for garnishing

Sour cream, for garnishing, optional

DIRECTIONS

1. Remove the stems from the tomatoes with a paring knife. Place the tomatoes in a heatproof bowl, fill the bowl with boiling water, and soak the tomatoes for 2 to 3 minutes. Drain the tomatoes, rinse with cold water, and peel the skin off with a knife. Chop the tomatoes and set aside.

2. Heat the oil in a large pot over medium heat. Add the onion and garlic and cook, stirring, until softened, about 3 minutes.

3. Add the broth or water, cabbage, beet, carrot, potatoes, bay leaves, and tomatoes. Bring to a boil, then lower the heat and allow to simmer, uncovered, until the veggies are tender, 15 to 20 minutes.

4. Remove the pot from the heat and stir in the parsley, salt, and pepper. Taste and adjust the salt and pepper as desired.

5. Garnish each serving with a sprinkling of dill and/or a dollop of sour cream, if desired.

+ Gluten-Free
+ Grain-Free
+ Sugar-Free
+ Soy-Free
+ Plant-Based
+ Nut-Free

Active time: 5 minutes
Total time: 35 minutes
Serves: 1

RAW LEMON-CARROT SOUP

INGREDIENTS

1 cup chopped carrot

1/2 cup chopped cabbage

1 cup water

1 tablespoon olive oil

Juiced one small lemon

1/2 teaspoon salt

1 teaspoon chopped dill

DIRECTIONS

1. Combine the carrot, cabbage, water, oil, lemon juice, and salt in a food processor or blender and pulse until well blended. Chill to the desired temperature, about 30 minutes, then stir and garnish with the chopped dill before serving.

+ Gluten-Free
+ Grain-Free
+ Sugar-Free
+ Soy-Free
+ Plant-Based
+ Nut-Free

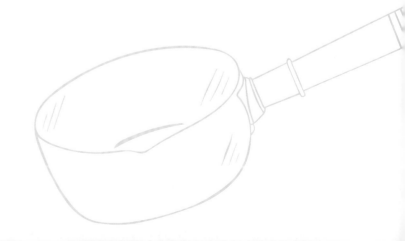

Active time: 5 minutes
Total time: 5 minutes
Serves: 1

CHILLED RAW BEET SOUP

INGREDIENTS

1/2 beet, peeled

1/2 lemon, peeled

1/3 cup chopped parsley

1 cup cold water

2 tablespoons olive oil

1 tablespoon parsley or cilantro for garnish, optional

DIRECTIONS

1. Combine the beet, lemon, parsley, water, and oil in a food processor or blender and pulse until well blended. Serve immediately, cold, topped with additional parsley or cilantro.

+ Gluten-Free
+ Grain-Free
+ Sugar-Free
+ Soy-Free
+ Plant-Based
+ Nut-Free
+ Raw/No-Bake

Active time: 15 minutes
Total time: 35 minutes
Serves: 4

I was recently speaking with a real estate agent who mentioned that because her daughter is vegan, she has had to seek out new and different recipes to accommodate her. With so many families following different lifestyles and diets, it's wonderful to have a few good plant-based recipes on hand for those who need them, and this stew recipe is perfect for vegans. That being said, this dish is so delicious and rich with flavor that everyone in your family will surely enjoy it, regardless of what they do or do not eat!

ZUCCHINI, CHICKPEA, AND TOMATO STEW

INGREDIENTS

3 large tomatoes

1/4 cup olive oil

1 medium onion, chopped

2 garlic cloves, thinly sliced

2 medium zucchini, chopped

2 teaspoons dried oregano

Sea salt, to taste

Black pepper, to taste

1 (15-ounce) can chickpeas, drained and rinsed

1/4 cup chopped parsley

2 cups cooked rice, quinoa, or pasta, for serving

Red pepper flakes, optional

DIRECTIONS

1. Remove the stems from the tomatoes with a paring knife. Place the tomatoes in a heatproof bowl, fill the bowl with boiling water, and soak the tomatoes for 2 to 3 minutes. Drain the tomatoes, rinse with cold water, and peel the skin off with a knife. Dice the tomatoes and set aside.

2. Heat the oil in a large skillet, add the onion and garlic, and cook, stirring, for 2 minutes, or until tender.

3. Stir in the tomatoes, lower the heat, and cook, stirring occasionally, for 13 minutes more.

4. Add the zucchini, oregano, salt, and pepper and cook for 6 more minutes, stirring occasionally.

5. Add the chickpeas and continue to cook until just heated through.

6. Stir in the parsley and serve alongside your favorite rice, quinoa, or pasta, topped with red pepper flakes, if desired.

+ Gluten-Free
+ Soy-Free
+ Sugar-Free
+ Plant-Based
+ Nut-Free

Active time: 15 minutes
Total time: 55 minutes
Serves: 4

This lentil soup is a very satisfying choice for any diet. I usually soak the lentils overnight before using them in this recipe, because it makes them much easier to digest and enhances the body's ability to soak up their nutrients. I like to serve this with fermented vegetables and feta cheese on the side.

SPROUTED LENTIL SOUP

INGREDIENTS

1 cup brown sprouted lentils, or regular brown lentils

3 tablespoons olive oil, plus additional for drizzling

1 onion, chopped

1 cup chopped celery

2 garlic cloves, diced

2 medium tomatoes, diced

1 teaspoons dried oregano

2 bay leaves

6 cups water or vegetable stock

1 cup washed and finely chopped kale

Sea salt to taste

Black pepper to taste

Apple cider vinegar, for drizzling

DIRECTIONS

1. If using regular brown lentils, the night before, place them in a large bowl, add enough water to cover well, and soak them overnight. Drain the water before proceeding with the recipe. (If you bought already-sprouted lentils, you can skip this step.)

2. Heat the 3 tablespoons oil in a large pot over low heat. Add the onions, celery, and garlic and cook, stirring, for about 3 minutes. Add the diced tomatoes and cook, stirring, for another 7 minutes.

3. Add the sprouted lentils, oregano, bay leaves, and water or vegetable stock and bring to a boil over high heat. Lower the heat, skim any scum off the top, then cover and simmer for 25 to 30 minutes, or until lentils are tender.

4. Add the chopped kale, salt, and pepper and cook for 5 more minutes, until the greens have softened.

5. Divide the soup among four bowls and drizzle each serving with 1 teaspoon of apple cider vinegar and a little olive oil.

+ Gluten-Free
+ Soy-Free
+ Sugar-Free
+ Nut-Free
+ Plant-based

Active time: 10 minutes
Total time: 25 minutes
Serves: 4

EASY SWEET POTATO SALAD

INGREDIENTS

4–5 sweet potatoes

1/2 cup chopped cilantro

1/4 cup chopped onion (about half a small onion)

1/3 cup olive oil

2 tablespoons apple cider vinegar

1/2 teaspoon salt

1/2 teaspoon black pepper

DIRECTIONS

1. Place the sweet potatoes in a large pot of water and bring to a boil over high heat. Boil the potatoes until fork-tender but not too soft, 14 to 18 minutes. Drain, rinse with cold water, and set aside.

2. Combine the cilantro, onion, oil, vinegar, salt, and pepper, and mix gently.

3. Cut the cooled potatoes into cubes, then transfer to a serving dish, drizzle with the dressing, and stir to combine well.

4. Serve immediately at room temperature, or chill to the desired temperature and serve cold.

+ Gluten-Free
+ Grain-Free
+ Sugar-Free
+ Soy-Free
+ Plant-Based
+ Nut-Free

Active time: 15 minutes
Total time: 1 hour
Serves: 4

BEET AND SPINACH SALAD

INGREDIENTS

3 beets, greens removed

4 ounces baby arugula

1/3 cup olive oil

Juiced 1 lemon

Pinch of salt, or more to taste

Pinch of freshly ground black pepper, or more to taste

1 cup feta or goat cheese crumbles

1/3 cup pine nuts

DIRECTIONS

1. Wash the beets, place in a pot, and add enough water to cover. Bring to a boil over high heat, then reduce to a simmer and cook for 40 to 45 minutes, until fork-tender. You want the beets to be tender but not too soft. Remove from the heat and drain the beets. When the beets are cool enough to handle, peel, slice, and set aside.

2. Place the arugula in a large bowl. Add the oil, lemon juice, salt, and pepper and mix until well coated. Add the beets, feta crumbles, and pine nuts and mix well before serving.

+ Gluten-Free
+ Grain-Free
+ Sugar-Free
+ Soy-Free
+ Vegetarian

This salad recipe takes less than ten minutes to throw together. It is simple and flavorful. It's a great side or starter dish, and I often eat this highly nutritious salad for lunch—it is very versatile and addicting! I hope you will love this salad as much as I do.

EASY YELLOW PAPAYA SALAD

INGREDIENTS

1/2 papaya, peeled and seeded

1/2 cup tahini

1/4 cup cacao nibs

1 tablespoon chia seeds

1 tablespoon hemp seeds, optional

DIRECTIONS

1. Slice the papaya widthwise into 1/2-inch-thick slices. Spoon the tahini over the papaya and sprinkle with the cacao nibs, chia seeds, and hemp seeds, if using.

+ Gluten-Free
+ Grain-Free
+ Sugar-Free
+ Soy-Free
+ Plant-Based
+ Nut-Free

Total time: 10 minutes
Serves: 4

YELLOW TOMATO WATERMELON SALAD

INGREDIENTS

4–5 cups seedless watermelon chunks (about 3 pounds)

1 1/2 pounds yellow heirloom tomatoes, diced

2 tablespoons chopped basil

3 tablespoons olive oil

1 teaspoon apple cider vinegar or lemon juice

1/2 teaspoon sea salt

2 1/2 cups arugula leaves

1 cup cubed feta cheese

DIRECTIONS

1. In a large bowl, combine the watermelon, tomatoes, basil, 2 tablespoons of the oil, the vinegar or lemon juice, and the salt.

2. In a separate bowl, toss the arugula with the remaining 1 tablespoon of oil. Divide the arugula among four serving plates, top with the watermelon salad, and serve with feta cheese cubes. Season to taste with more salt, if desired.

+ Gluten-Free
+ Grain-Free
+ Sugar-Free
+ Soy-Free
+ Vegetarian
+ Nut-Free

Total time: 10 minutes
Serves: 4

This simple salad comes together in no time, and makes a satisfying lunch or dinner.

KALE SEED SALAD

INGREDIENTS

1/3 cup olive oil

1/4 cup apple cider vinegar or lemon juice

1/2 teaspoon sea salt

1/2 teaspoon freshly ground black pepper

5 cups coarsely chopped kale, any tough stems removed

1/3 cup sliced tigernuts, raw or toasted

3 tablespoons sunflower seeds

3 tablespoons pepitas, raw or toasted

2 tablespoons hemp seeds, optional

DIRECTIONS

1. In a large bowl, combine the oil, vinegar or lemon juice, salt, and pepper and whisk together until well combined. Add the kale and toss to coat.

2. Add the tigernuts, sunflower seeds, pepitas, and hemp seeds, if using, and toss again before serving.

+ Gluten-Free
+ Grain-Free
+ Sugar-Free
+ Soy-Free
+ Plant-Based
+ Raw/No-Bake
+ Nut-Free

Enjoy this avocado toast on its own, or serve it alongside poached or fried eggs and a baby arugula or mixed-green salad.

AVOCADO TOAST

INGREDIENTS

2 ripe avocados, peeled and pits removed

2 tablespoons fresh lemon juice

1/2 teaspoon ground cumin

1/2 teaspoon black pepper

Pinch of salt

4 slices gluten-free bread, home-made (page 93) or store-bought, toasted

2 tablespoons olive oil

1 tablespoon chia or hemp seeds

1/2 teaspoon red pepper flakes

Optional Toppings:

Pepitas (pumpkin seeds)

Sunflower seeds

Goat cheese crumbles

DIRECTIONS

1. In a small bowl, combine the avocado, lemon juice, cumin, black pepper, and salt, and gently mash with the back of a fork.

2. Divide the mashed avocado mixture evenly on top of the toasted bread slices, drizzle with olive oil, and sprinkle the chia or hemp seeds and red pepper flakes over the top. Add a sprinkle of pepitas, sunflower seeds, and/or goat cheese before serving, if desired.

+ Gluten-Free
+ Refined Sugar-Free
+ Soy-Free
+ Plant-Based (Option)
+ Nut-Free

BITTER HERBS SALAD

INGREDIENTS

1/4 cup olive oil

3 tablespoons apple cider vinegar or fresh lemon juice

1/2 teaspoon black pepper

Salt to taste

3 ounces mixed greens, such as arugula, mustard, baby kale, and mitzuna

1 large handful parsley leaves, roughly chopped

1 large handful cilantro leaves, roughly chopped

1 large handful fresh tarragon, chopped

1/4 cup dill fronds, roughly chopped

4 radishes, chopped

1 (8-ounce) ball fresh burrata mozzarella

DIRECTIONS

1. In a large bowl, combine the oil, vinegar or lemon juice, black pepper, and salt and whisk together until well combined.

2. Add the mixed greens, herbs, and radishes and toss to coat.
Divide the salad among four plates, cut the cheese into quarters, and top each salad with a burrata wedge.

+ Gluten-Free
+ Grain-Free
+ Sugar-Free
+ Soy+Free
+ Vegetarian
+ Nut-Free

+ MAIN DISHES FOR VEGETARIANS AND MEAT LOVERS

Total time: 15 minutes
Serves: 4

My stomach is very sensitive and I try to make everything homemade with fresh and wholesome ingredients. This basil pesto can be used with various meals. This recipe is for zucchini noodles with pesto, but you can also use this sauce to top any type of pasta, chicken, fish, or veggies. This dish can be made raw or cooked and can be served cold, room temperature, or warm. My preference is to cook the noodles and serve warm.

ZUCCHINI NOODLES WITH BASIL PESTO

INGREDIENTS

FOR THE BASIL PESTO:

1 large handful of basil (about 2 cups)

1/2 cup tigernut flour

1 or 2 garlic cloves, peeled

1 cup olive oil, plus more to taste

1/2 teaspoon sea salt, or to taste

FOR THE ZUCCHINI NOODLES:

3 large zucchini

Fresh basil leaves, for garnishing

Halved cherry tomatoes, for garnishing, optional

Parmesan cheese or vegan parmesan, for sprinkling, optional

DIRECTIONS

1. To make the pesto: Place the basil, tigernut flour, garlic cloves, olive oil, and salt in a food processor or high-speed blender and pulse until a smooth paste forms. Taste and add more salt and/or oil as needed.

2. To make the zucchini noodles: Spiralize the zucchini with a spiralizer. Toss the raw zucchini with the pesto until well coated. Or, if you prefer to cook your zucchini noodles, toss the pesto and zucchini noodles together, then transfer to a skillet over medium heat and sauté for a few minutes.

3. Garnish with basil leaves, halved cherry tomatoes, and a sprinkle of vegan or regular parmesan cheese, if using, and serve warm, at room temperature, or chilled.

+ Gluten-Free
+ Grain-Free
+ Sugar-Free
+ Soy-Free
+ Plant-Based (Option)
+ Nut-Free

Active time: 10 minutes
Total time: 30 minutes
Serves: 6

These herb-stuffed mushrooms are simple to make and truly delicious. The portobello mushrooms are perfect for a healthy, low-carb family dinner, and they also make a great plant-based dish for an elegant party.

PESTO-STUFFED PORTOBELLO MUSHROOMS

INGREDIENTS

6 portobello mushrooms

1/3 cup olive oil

2 cups fresh basil leaves, plus additional for garnishing

1 cup parsley leaves

1/2 cup tigernut flour

1/2 teaspoon salt

1/2 teaspoon ground pepper

Chile pepper flakes, optional, for garnishing

DIRECTIONS

1. Preheat the oven to 350°F and line a baking sheet with parchment paper.

2. Remove the stems from the portobello mushroom caps. Wash the caps and dry with a paper towel.

3. Brush both sides of the mushrooms with half of the oil, and place the mushrooms stem-cavity side up on the prepared baking sheet.

4. Combine the basil, parsley, tigernut flour, salt, pepper, and remaining oil in a food processor, and pulse until combined. Divide the stuffing among the mushrooms, spooning it into each stem cavity to fill.

5. Bake for 20 to 25 minutes, or until the mushrooms are cooked and the stuffing is golden. Garnish with basil leaves and sprinkle with the chile flakes, if using, before serving.

+ Gluten-Free
+ Grain-Free
+ Sugar-Free
+ Soy-Free
+ Plant-Based
+ Nut-Free

Active time: 10 minutes
Total time: 45 minutes
Serves: 4

This is a traditional dish from my home country, the Republic of Georgia. While in Georgia, we would use sour plums for this recipe, I've had a hard time finding sour plums in my local New York market. Instead, I use lime or lemon juice for the sour flavor, along with a combination of fresh herbs that give this dish its amazing balance.

CHAKAPULI (LAMB AND TARRAGON STEW)

INGREDIENTS

2 pounds boneless lamb stew meat

1 small onion, chopped

1 cup white wine

3 1/2 cups water

1 bunch scallions, chopped (both white and green parts)

1 bunch parsley, chopped

1 bunch cilantro, chopped

1 cup chopped tarragon leaves

1/4 cup chopped dill (about 1/4 bunch)

3 garlic cloves, minced

Juice of 1 lime or lemon

Sea salt to taste

DIRECTIONS

1. Combine the beef, onion, and wine in a large pot over low heat and cook, stirring occasionally, for 10 minutes.

2. Add the water, scallions, parsley, cilantro, tarragon, dill, and garlic and cook, covered, for 30 minutes, stirring occasionally. Add the citrus juice and salt and serve with white rice, or cauliflower rice for a grain-free option.

+ Gluten-Free
+ Grain-Free (Option)
+ Sugar-Free
+ Soy-Free
+ Nut-Free
+ Dairy-Free

Active time: 10 minutes
Total time: 35 minutes
Serves: 4–6

This homemade tomato sauce with mushrooms goes well with any type of pasta. I prefer to always use homemade sauces, not only because they taste better, but also because I am never sure how my body will react to store-bought sauces, which usually contain preservatives and additives.

PASTA WITH MUSHROOM-TOMATO SAUCE

INGREDIENTS

3 large beefsteak tomatoes

8 ounces cremini mushrooms, sliced (about 3 cups)

2 1/2 teaspoons salt, or to taste

12 ounces gluten-free spaghetti (or any other variety of pasta)

1/4 cup olive oil

1 small onion, chopped

2 garlic cloves, minced

1 teaspoon oregano

1/2 teaspoon ground black pepper

1 bay leaf

1/4 cup chopped fresh parsley

DIRECTIONS

1. Remove the stems from the tomatoes with a paring knife. Place the tomatoes in a heatproof bowl, fill the bowl with boiling water, and soak the tomatoes for 2 to 3 minutes. Drain, rinse with cold water, and peel the skin off with a knife.

2. Dice the peeled tomatoes and transfer to a bowl, then add the mushrooms and set aside.

3. Fill a large pot with water, season with 2 teaspoons of the salt, and bring to a boil. Add the gluten-free spaghetti and cook according to the directions on the box.

4. Meanwhile, heat the oil in a large saucepan over medium heat. Add the onion and garlic and cook until golden-brown, about 3 minutes, then add the tomatoes, mushrooms, oregano, the remaining 1/2 teaspoon salt, the pepper, and the bay leaf. Cover the pan and bring to a low simmer. Cook for 25 to 30 minutes.

5. Remove the bay leaf, stir in the chopped parsley, and serve over the cooked pasta.

+ Gluten-Free
+ Soy+Free
+ Plant-Based
+ Nut-Free

Active time: 10 minutes
Total time: 30 minutes
Serves: 4–6

SPINACH RICE

INGREDIENTS

1/3 cup olive oil

1 medium onion, chopped

1/4 cup chopped leek

2 garlic cloves, minced

3 cups water

1 cup uncooked white rice

4–5 ounces baby spinach

1 teaspoon salt

1 teaspoon ground black pepper

Chopped fresh dill, for garnishing

Chopped fresh cilantro, optional, for garnishing

DIRECTIONS

1. Heat the oil in a large sauté pan over medium-low heat. Add the onion, leek, and garlic and cook, stirring, until softened, about 3 minutes.

2. Add the water and bring it to a boil. Stir in the rice, reduce the heat to medium-low, and simmer for 14 minutes.

3. Slowly stir in the baby spinach, salt, and pepper and cook for about 4 minutes more. If the rice seems dry, add up to 1 cup more hot water as needed.

4. Remove from the heat and let sit, covered, for 5 minutes. Sprinkle with the chopped dill and cilantro, if using, before serving.

+ Gluten-Free
+ Sugar-Free
+ Soy-Free
+ Plant-Based
+ Nut-Free

Active time: 10 minutes
Total time: 30 minutes
Serves: 4–6

This quick and easy recipe is a vegetarian's delight! If you are a mushroom lover, this dish is perfect for you and your family. The tender and caramelized cremini mushrooms make it very flavorful. You can serve this as a side or as a main, and pair it with just about anything.

RICE WITH MUSHROOMS

INGREDIENTS

1/3 cup olive oil or butter

12 ounces cremini mushrooms, coarsely chopped

1 large onion, finely chopped

2 garlic cloves, minced

1 cup uncooked white rice

2 1/2 cups water

1 teaspoon salt

1 handful of fresh parsley, chopped

1/2 teaspoon black pepper

DIRECTIONS

1. Heat the oil or butter in a large sauté pan over medium heat. Add the mushrooms, onion, and garlic, cook, stirring, until the mushrooms have released their liquid and the liquid has evaporated.

2. Add the rice, water, and salt, lower the heat to medium-low, and cook, covered, for 18 minutes, until the rice is fully cooked. If the rice seems dry, add more hot water as needed.

3. Stir in the parsley and black pepper before serving.

+ Gluten-Free
+ Sugar-Free
+ Soy-Free
+ Plant-Based
+ Nut-Free

Active time: 15 minutes
Total time: 25 minutes
Serves: 4

This is a perfect dinner dish—healthy and packed with flavor. You can add these meatballs to your favorite pasta sauce, or enjoy them as an appetizer. They are also great served with mashed cauliflower, with your favorite sauce drizzled on top.

TURKEY MEATBALLS

INGREDIENTS

1 pound ground turkey

1 large egg

1/2 cup thinly chopped onion

1/2 cup freshly grated Parmesan cheese

2 tablespoons chopped parsley

1 tablespoon ground black pepper

1/2 cup cassava or oat flour

1/2 cup olive oil

DIRECTIONS

1. In a large bowl, combine the turkey, egg, onion, Parmesan, parsley, and pepper and mix together with your hands or a wooden spoon until well combined.

2. Place the cassava flour on a plate or in a shallow bowl. Using your hands, shape the meat mixture into golf-ball-sized meatballs and dip them into the cassava flour, rolling to coat on all sides.

3. Heat the oil in a large skillet over medium heat. Add the meatballs and cook for about 5 minutes on each side, until crispy and brown. Serve as-is with a side dish, or add to your favorite pasta sauce.

+ Gluten-Free
+ Grain-Free (Option)
+ Sugar-Free
+ Soy-Free
+ Nut-Free

Active time: 10 minutes
Total time: 45 minutes
Serves: 4

This traditional Georgian recipe reminds me of my childhood. I always use fresh tomatoes and peel them before chopping, because it makes them easier for the body to digest; if you prefer, however, you can use canned chopped tomatoes instead.

CHAKHOKHBILI (CHICKEN WITH TOMATOES AND HERBS)

INGREDIENTS

4 large tomatoes

1/4 cup butter

1 1/2 pounds skin-on, bone-in chicken pieces (thighs, legs, and/ or breasts)

1 large onion, chopped

1/4 cup chopped parsley

1/4 cup chopped cilantro

2 tablespoons chopped dill

1 tablespoon salt

1/2 teaspoon black pepper

DIRECTIONS

1. Remove the stems from the tomatoes with a paring knife. Place the tomatoes in a heatproof bowl, fill the bowl with boiling water, and soak the tomatoes for 2 to 3 minutes. Drain the tomatoes, rinse with cold water, and peel the skin off with a knife. Dice the tomatoes and set aside.

2. Heat the butter in a large, heavy-bottomed pot over high heat. When the butter is melted, add the chicken pieces and chopped onion and cook, turning occasionally, until browned on all sides.

3. Add the tomatoes and stir. Lower the heat to medium and cook for about 30 minutes.

4. Remove from the heat and stir in the parsley, cilantro, dill, salt, and pepper. Let stand, covered, for 5 minutes before serving.

5. Serve hot with rice, bread, or cauliflower rice.

+ Gluten-Free
+ Grain-Free
+ Sugar-Free
+ Soy-Free
+ Nut-Free

Active time: 10 minutes
Total time: 20 minutes
Serves: 4

This is a classic Georgian or Russian-style recipe. The traditional version is made with wheat flour, but I love making a gluten-free version with almond flour. You can also replace the almond flour with tigernut or oat flour.

BEEF PATTIES

INGREDIENTS

1 1/2 pounds ground beef

1 medium onion, finely chopped or grated

1 egg

2 tablespoons finely chopped parsley

1 tablespoon dried oregano

1/2 teaspoon salt

1/2 teaspoon ground pepper

1/2 cup almond flour

2–3 tablespoons olive oil

DIRECTIONS

1. In a large bowl, combine the beef, onion, egg, parsley, oregano, salt, and pepper and mix together with your hands until well combined.

2. Place the almond flour on a plate or in a shallow bowl. Using your hands, divide the mixture into golf-ball-sized portions, shape them into oval patties, and dip each one into the almond flour, making sure they are covered with flour on all sides.

3. Heat the oil in a large skillet over medium heat. Add the patties and cook for about 5 minutes on each side, until browned and cooked through. Serve with buckwheat or rice, or with vegetables for a grain-free option.

+ Gluten-Free
+ Grain-Free (Option)
+ Soy-Free
+ Dairy-Free
+ Sugar-Free

Active time: 10 minutes
Total time: 55 minutes
Serves: 6

This is a traditional soup from my birth country, the Republic of Georgia, and a perfect dinner idea for a cozy evening at home. I grew up eating this soup, and to this day, the aroma of borscht filling my apartment brings back fond memories of my childhood.

BORSCHT WITH BEEF

INGREDIENTS

1 pound bone-in or boneless sirloin beef

13 cups water

4 large fresh tomatoes

1/3 cup olive oil

1 large onion, finely diced

3 garlic cloves, chopped

2 medium russet potatoes, peeled and chopped

2 cups sliced cabbage

3 small beets, washed, peeled, and grated

1 large carrot, grated

2 bay leaves

1/4 cup chopped fresh parsley

1 teaspoon salt, or more to taste

1/2 teaspoon ground black pepper, or more to taste

1/4 cup chopped fresh dill

6 tablespoons sour cream, optional

+ Gluten-Free
+ Grain-Free
+ Soy-Free
+ Nut-Free
+ Dairy-Free
+ Sugar-Free

DIRECTIONS

1. Wash the beef and place in a large soup pot, then add the water. Bring to a boil and skim the foam off the top as it boils. Lower the heat and cook, partially covered, for about 30 minutes.

2. Remove the stems from the tomatoes with a paring knife. Place the tomatoes in a heatproof bowl, fill the bowl with boiling water, and soak the tomatoes for 2 to 3 minutes. Drain the tomatoes, rinse with cold water, and peel the skin off with a knife. Dice the tomatoes and set aside.

3. Meanwhile, heat the oil in a small skillet over medium heat. Add the onion and garlic and cook, stirring, for about 3 minutes.

4. Once the meat has been cooking for at least 30 minutes, add the tomatoes and potatoes. Continue to cook for another 5 minutes, then add the onions and garlic, cabbage, beets, carrot, and bay leaves, and cook for 10 minutes more.

5. Remove the pot from the heat. Stir in the parsley, salt, and pepper, then taste and adjust the salt and pepper as desired.

6. Serve each portion with a sprinkling of dill and a tablespoon of sour cream, if desired.

Active time: 10 minutes
Total time: 45 minutes
Serves: 6

This traditional dish from the Republic of Georgia is usually made with white wheat flour, but my gluten-free version substitutes cassava flour and still tastes just like the original. Every time I make this dish, I am reminded of my childhood. I hope you and your kids will enjoy it as much as my family does.

CHIKHITMA (GEORGIAN CHICKEN EGG DROP SOUP)

INGREDIENTS

1 large whole chicken, or about 2 1/2 pounds mixed bone-in chicken parts

8 1/2 cups water, divided

1 large onion, chopped

3 cloves garlic, minced

3 tablespoons cassava flour

3 large eggs, beaten

1/4 chopped cilantro

2 tablespoons chopped dill

Sea salt and black pepper to taste

2 tablespoons apple cider vinegar, optional, for serving

DIRECTIONS

1. Place the chicken in a large pot, add 8 cups water, and bring the water to a simmer. As it simmers, skim any foam that rises to the top and discard. Cover and simmer for about 30 minutes, or until chicken is well done. Remove the chicken from the broth, leaving the broth on the heat. When the chicken is cool enough to handle, remove the meat from the bones and set aside.

2. Add the onion and garlic to the broth and simmer for 2 minutes. In a small cup, combine the cassava flour and 1/4 cup cold water and stir to dissolve the cassava flour; pour into the broth and simmer for another 2 minutes.

3. Reduce the heat to low. In another small cup, use a fork to beat the eggs together with 1/4 cup cold water, then pour the egg slowly into the broth. Stir gently while pouring the egg, then remove from the heat.

4. Add the cilantro, dill, sea salt, pepper, and chicken meat to the broth. Divide among bowls, drizzle each serving with 1 teaspoon of the apple cider vinegar, if desired, and serve.

+ Gluten-Fre
+ Grain-Free
+ Soy-Free
+ Nut-Free
+ Dairy-Free
+ Sugar-Free

Active time: 10 minutes
Total time: 30 minutes
Serves: 4

I developed a love for crusted chicken after I moved to the United States; however, every chicken cutlet I tried in restaurants was made with wheat flour. This is my healthy, nutritious, and grain-free version. I strive to make all my recipes healthier versions of the classics they're based on, which usually means finding gluten-free alternatives that don't diminish the taste of the original. Tigernut flour has been immensely helpful in this regard, since it is actually a root vegetable that tastes like a carbohydrate and that soaks up a variety of flavors.

TIGERNUT-CRUSTED CHICKEN CUTLETS

INGREDIENTS

1 1/2 pounds thinly sliced chicken breast

1 teaspoon salt, plus additional for sprinkling

1 3/4 cups tigernut flour

3 large eggs

3/4 cup grated Parmesan cheese

1 teaspoon ground paprika

1 teaspoon black pepper

1/2 teaspoon garlic powder

1/3 cup olive oil or ghee, or more as needed, for frying

DIRECTIONS

1. Lay out the chicken on a cutting board, baking sheet, or plate and sprinkle it all over with salt, then sprinkle with about 1/2 cup of the tigernut flour.

2. Beat the eggs in a small bowl and set aside. In another bowl, mix the remaining 1 1/4 cups tigernut flour with the Parmesan, paprika, black pepper, garlic powder, and 1 teaspoon of salt.

3. Dip each piece of chicken in the eggs to coat. Let the excess drip off, then coat in the tigernut flour-Parmesan mixture and set aside. Repeat with the remaining chicken.

4. Heat the olive oil or ghee in a large skillet over medium-high heat. Add half the chicken slices and cook until golden on one side, 3 to 4 minutes. Flip and cook on the other side for 3 to 4 minutes. Transfer to a paper towel-lined plate and repeat with the remaining chicken slices, adding more oil to the pan if needed. Serve immediately.

+ Gluten-Free
+ Grain-Free
+ Soy-Free
+ Nut-Free
+ Sugar-Free

Active time: 10 minutes
Total time: 30 minutes
Serves: 4

This recipe takes traditional chicken tenders and makes them healthier using grain-free and highly nutritious oatmeal flour. While using a cast-iron pan is ideal for fried chicken, you can also substitute any good skillet that controls heat well.

FRIED CHICKEN TENDERS

INGREDIENTS

Olive oil or ghee, for frying

1 3/4 cups gluten-free oatmeal flour

2 tablespoons turmeric

1 tablespoon dried oregano

1 teaspoon ground paprika

1 teaspoon salt

1 teaspoon black pepper

1/2 teaspoon garlic powder

3 large eggs

1 1/2 pounds chicken breast, thinly sliced into tenders

DIRECTIONS

1. Fill a skillet with about 2 inches of oil or ghee and place over medium-high heat.

2. While the oil heats up, bread your chicken tenders: In a large mixing bowl, combine the flour, turmeric, oregano, paprika, salt, pepper, and garlic powder.

3. In another bowl, beat the eggs.

4. Dip each piece of chicken in the flour mixture to coat, then dip in the egg, let any excess drip off, and dip in the flour mixture again.

5. Fry the breaded chicken a few pieces at a time for 3 minutes on each side. Transfer to a paper towel-lined plate and repeat with the remaining chicken. Serve immediately.

+ Gluten-Free
+ Soy-Free
+ Nut-Free
+ Dairy-Free
+ Sugar-Free

Active time: 15 minutes
Total time : 40 minutes
Serves: 4

Gupta is one of my favorite childhood soup recipes. With its protein-packed meatballs and dense texture, it makes a truly hearty meal. I serve this soup as a main course to high praise from my family and friends, who often request a second or even third serving.

GUPTA (MEATBALL SOUP)

INGREDIENTS

1 large tomato

1/4 cup olive oil

1/2 onion, chopped

1 garlic clove, minced

6 cups water

1 pound ground beef

1/2 cup uncooked white rice

2 tablespoons dried oregano

2 teaspoons sea salt

1 teaspoon ground black pepper

1/4 cup chopped cilantro

2 tablespoons chopped dill

DIRECTIONS

1. Remove the stem from the tomato with a paring knife. Place the tomato in a heatproof bowl, then fill the bowl with boiling water and soak the tomato for 2 to 3 minutes. Rinse with cold water, peel the skin off with a knife, and dice the tomato.

2. Heat the olive oil in a large pot over medium heat. Add the onion and garlic and cook, stirring, for 2 minutes. Add the diced tomatoes and continue to cook for 3 more minutes. Pour in the water and bring to a boil.

3. In a large bowl, combine the ground beef, rice, oregano, 1 teaspoon of the salt, and the pepper and mix with your hands until well combined. Start making the meat mixture into small balls, and drop each one straight into the boiling water. When you have finished adding all the meatballs, cover the pot, reduce the heat to low and simmer covered for 20 minutes.

4. Remove from the heat, add the cilantro, dill, and the remaining 1 teaspoon sea salt, and serve hot.

+ Gluten-Free
+ Soy-Free
+ Sugar-Free
+ Nut-Free
+ Dairy-Free

Active time: 5 minutes
Total time: 50 minutes
Serves: 4–6

Cilantro and lime contribute a bright, fresh flavor to this baked chicken. A dependable weeknight recipe that's healthy, hearty, and easy to tweak with your own substitutions, this is a great choice for family dinners, and goes well with rice or vegetables. I can eat this dish two or three times a week and never get tired of it!

BAKED CILANTRO-LIME CHICKEN

INGREDIENTS

Juice of 2 limes

1/3 cup olive oil

1 cup cilantro

2 garlic cloves

1 1/2 teaspoons sea salt

6–8 skin-on, bone-in chicken pieces (thighs and breasts)

DIRECTIONS

1. Combine the lime juice, olive oil, cilantro, garlic, and salt in a food processor and process for less than 1 minute to blend well.

2. Place the chicken in a large bowl, pour the marinade over the chicken, and gently massage it with your hands until all of the chicken pieces are thoroughly coated. Refrigerate the chicken in the marinade for at least 2 hours and up to 24 hours.

3. Preheat the oven to 400°F.

4. Remove the chicken from the fridge and transfer it to a baking pan, then pour any remaining marinade over the top. Arrange the chicken pieces skin side up in the pan, leaving some room in between each piece.

5. Bake, uncovered, for about 45 minutes, or until the chicken's internal temperature reads 165 to 170°F on a meat thermometer.

6. Remove the chicken from the oven and let it rest for about 5 minutes. Serve it with rice, with any extra juice from the pan drizzled on top.

+ Gluten-Free
+ Grain-Free
+ Soy-Free
+ Sugar-Free
+ Nut-Free
+ Dairy-Free

Total time: 25 minutes
Serves: 4

Turmeric has become one of my favorite spices over the last six years, and its flavor goes especially well with this shrimp salad recipe. Turmeric has a wide range of health benefits—in fact, I often turn to turmeric pills, as well as turmeric tea with ginger and black pepper, to help when I have any kind of body ache or feel myself coming down with a common cold.

WARM TURMERIC SHRIMP SALAD

INGREDIENTS

FOR THE SHRIMP

3 tablespoons olive oil

3 tablespoons lime juice

2 tablespoons ground turmeric

1 teaspoon garlic powder

1 teaspoon sea salt

1/2 teaspoon ground black pepper

1 pound large shrimp, cleaned and deveined

3 tablespoons butter

FOR THE SALAD

1/4 cup olive oil

3 tablespoons apple cider vinegar

Pinch of sea salt

8 ounces baby spinach

1 avocado, peeled, pitted, and chopped

1/4 cup hemp seeds

DIRECTIONS

1. To make the shrimp: Combine the oil, lime juice, turmeric, garlic powder, salt, and pepper in a large bowl and mix well with a whisk. Add the shrimp and mix until well coated with the sauce.

2. Melt the butter in a large skillet over medium heat. Add the coated shrimp and any excess turmeric sauce and cook, stirring, for 9 minutes. Remove from the heat and set aside.

3. To make the salad: In a medium bowl, whisk together the olive oil, apple cider vinegar, and sea salt. Add the spinach, avocado, and hemp seeds, toss gently, and serve with the shrimp.

+ Gluten-Free
+ Grain-Free
+ Soy-Free
+ Sugar-Free
+ Nut-Free

Active time: 20 minutes
Total time: 30 minutes
Serves: 4

This cod curry dish is simple to make and packed with flavor, which makes it perfect any evening for a family dinner. The cod complements the curry flavor well, and the easy recipe requires less than 20 minutes of active time.

COD, MUSHROOM, AND COCONUT CURRY STEW

INGREDIENTS

1/4 cup olive oil

2 garlic cloves, crushed

1 tablespoon fresh grated ginger

2 tablespoons curry powder

8 ounces mixed enoki and beech mushrooms, or 8 ounces shiitake mushrooms

1 cup coconut milk

Sea salt to taste

1 pound cod fillets, cut into 2-inch pieces

2 large handfuls baby spinach (about 5 ounces)

DIRECTIONS

1. Heat the oil in a skillet over medium heat. Add the garlic, ginger, and curry powder and cook, stirring, for about 2 minutes.

2. Add the mushrooms and cook, stirring, for 4 to 6 minutes.

3. Pour in the coconut milk and salt. Add the fish chunks and stir, then cover with a tight-fitting lid and simmer for 10 minutes. Try to avoid aggressive stirring once the fish is in, as it will break apart.

4. Gently stir in the spinach and simmer for 3 minutes more.

5. Serve with white rice or brown rice.

+ Gluten-Free
+ Dairy-Free
+ Soy-Free
+ Sugar-Free

Active time: 15 minutes
Total time: 1 hour 15 minutes
Serves: 4

This is my gluten-free version of a popular Greek pie. My partner in life and business is Greek, and when we traveled together to Greece, I quickly found that the Greek culture inspired me—not only the people and the island, but also the nature, the colors, and even the weather!

While I think it is important to eat healthfully, I don't believe that doing so has to mean sacrificing good flavor—and this recipe proves my point! The pie is exquisite in taste and full of essential nutrients. It also happens to be easy to prepare, and is one of my family's favorite dishes. I make this often for dinner and, without fail, it disappears almost as soon as it hits the table.

CRUSTLESS ZUCCHINI MINT PIE

INGREDIENTS

3 large eggs, beaten

3/4 cup milk

2 1/2 cups shredded zucchini, all liquid squeezed out (about 3 medium zucchini)

2 cups chopped mint

3/4 cup gluten-free oat or amaranth flour

1/4 cup arrowroot flour

1 3/4 cups cubed feta cheese

1/4 cup olive oil

DIRECTIONS

1. Preheat the oven to 350°F. Line two 9-inch pie plates or one 13-x-9-inch baking dish with parchment paper and lightly spray with cooking spray.

2. In a small bowl, combine the eggs, milk, zucchini, mint, oat or amaranth flour, and arrowroot flour and mix until well combined. Fold in the feta cheese and mix well. Pour into the prepared pie plates or baking dish, drizzle the olive oil on top, and bake for 50 to 60 minutes, until slightly browned. Let cool in the pan for 15 to 20 minutes, then cut into wedges for serving.

+ Gluten-Free
+ Sugar-Free
+ Vegetarian
+ Soy-Free
+ Nut-Free

Active time: 15 minutes
Total time: 1 hour 5 minutes
Serves: 4

I am elated to share this incredibly delicious recipe with you, as it has always been a favorite of mine. Cauliflower rice offers a fresh, healthy twist on the traditional white rice for a low-carb meal. If you are a rice lover, you can replace the cauliflower rice with sprouted brown or white rice, or serve the cauliflower-rice-stuffed peppers atop a bowl of brown or white rice to enjoy both—the rice and its cauliflower counterpart—together.

STUFFED PEPPERS WITH CAULIFLOWER RICE

INGREDIENTS

8 bell peppers, mixed colors

1/2 head of cauliflower, about 1 1/2 cup

1/4 cup olive oil

1 pound ground beef

1 small eggplant, finely chopped

1 medium onion, finely chopped

2 garlic cloves, finely chopped

2 large tomatoes, diced

1 tablespoon dried oregano

1 teaspoon salt

1/2 (4-ounce) can tomato sauce

1 cup shredded mozzarella cheese

DIRECTIONS

1. Preheat the oven to 375°F. Grease or spray a 9-x-13-inch baking dish with olive oil.

2. Wash the peppers and cut off the tops. Remove and discard the stems and seeds; chop and reserve the pepper tops. Arrange the bell peppers standing up in the prepared baking dish.

3. Pulse the cauliflower in a food processor until it is broken down into rice-sized pieces.

4. Heat the oil in a large pan over medium-high heat. Add the ground beef, eggplant, onion, garlic, and chopped pepper tops and cook, stirring and breaking up the beef with a wooden spoon, until no longer pink, about 5 minutes. Add diced tomatoes, cauliflower rice, oregano, and salt and cook for another 3 minutes.

5. Divide the stuffing evenly among the peppers. Pour the tomato sauce over the peppers.

6. Cover with foil and bake for 30 minutes, then uncover and sprinkle with the cheese. Return to the oven and bake for 20 more minutes. Serve the stuffed peppers on their own or with brown or white rice.

+ Gluten-Free
+ Grain-Free
+ Soy-Free
+ Sugar-Free
+ Nut-Free

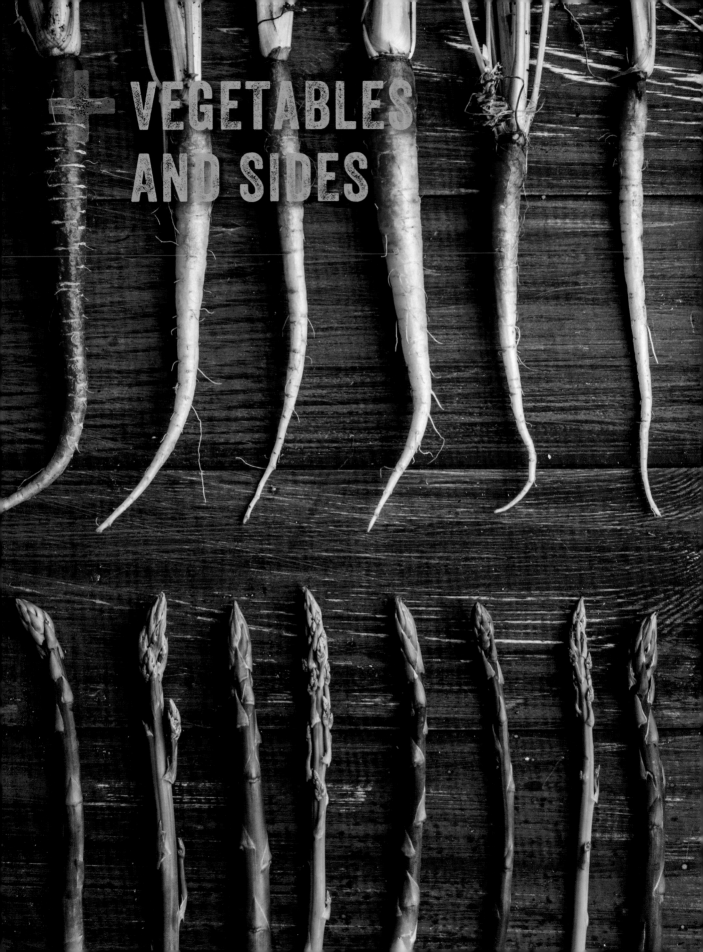

VEGETABLES
AND SIDES

+ Roasted Carrots with Creamy Sauce

+ Oven-Roasted Asparagus

+ Long-Grain White Rice

+ Cauliflower Rice with Herbs

+ Black Rice with Herbs

+ Buckwheat with Ghee

+ Quinoa with Lemon Juice

+ Brown Rice with Walnuts

No matter what main dish you are having, there is a perfect side in here for you. These simple, easy-to-prepare side dishes will complete any meal and save you time and energy. Or skip the main dish altogether—sometimes all you have to do to create a balanced, nutritious meal is put a few sides together!

Active time: 10 minutes
Total time: 40 minutes
Serves: 4

Enjoy these carrots simply roasted on their own, or paired with the creamy sauce.

ROASTED CARROTS WITH CREAMY SAUCE

INGREDIENTS

2 bunches carrots (about 16 small carrots)

1/3 cup olive oil

2 tablespoons fresh lemon juice

1 tablespoon grated lemon zest

1/2 teaspoon salt

1/2 teaspoon black pepper

FOR THE SAUCE

1/2 cup peeled tigernuts

3/4 cup water

1/4 cup fresh lemon juice

3 tablespoons olive oil

1 teaspoon dried coriander

1/2 teaspoon cayenne pepper

1/2 teaspoon ground cumin

1/2 teaspoon black pepper

1/8 teaspoon salt

1 garlic clove, optional

1 tablespoon nutritional yeast, optional

DIRECTIONS

1. To begin the sauce: Soak the tigernuts in water for at least 8 hours, or up to 24 hours.

2. To make the carrots: Preheat the oven to 425°F.

3. Trim the carrot tops off and wash the carrots well, leaving them unpeeled. Place the carrots in a baking dish and drizzle with the olive oil and lemon juice. Mix to completely coat the carrots, then sprinkle with the lemon zest, salt, and pepper.

4. Bake for about 30 minutes. Let cool before serving.

5. Meanwhile, to make the sauce: Transfer the tigernuts and their soaking liquid to a food processor or high speed blender, add, lemon juice, oil, coriander, cayenne, cumin, black pepper, salt, and garlic and nutritional yeast, if using, and pulse until well blended. Chill to the desired temperature and drizzle on top of the cooled carrots. Devour immediately.

+ Gluten-Free
+ Grain-Free
+ Sugar-Free
+ Soy-Free
+ Plant-Based
+ Nut-Free

Active time: 10 minutes
Total time: 25 minutes
Serves: 4

Here is the best way you can roast asparagus. You will want to make this melt-in-your-mouth feta-asparagus dish for family dinners, holiday meals, or on any given evening!

OVEN-ROASTED ASPARAGUS

INGREDIENTS

1 bunch asparagus, tough ends trimmed

1/4 cup olive oil

Juice of 1 small lemon

1 teaspoon dried oregano

1/2 teaspoon salt

1/2 teaspoon ground black pepper

1 cup cubed feta cheese

DIRECTIONS

1. Preheat the oven to 425°F.

2. Place the asparagus in a baking dish and drizzle with the olive oil and lemon juice. Mix to completely coat the asparagus, then sprinkle with the oregano, salt, pepper, and feta.

3. Bake for 13 minutes, or until the asparagus is done to your liking.

+ Gluten-Free
+ Grain-Free
+ Sugar-Free
+ Soy-Free
+ Nut-Free
+ Vegetarian

Active time: 5 minutes
Total time: 30 minutes
Serves: 4

LONG-GRAIN WHITE RICE

INGREDIENTS

1 cup long-grain white rice

2 cups water

2 tablespoons ghee or butter

Pinch of sea salt

DIRECTIONS

1. Rinse the rice. In a small saucepan, bring the water to a boil. Add the rice, ghee or butter, and salt. Lower the heat and simmer, covered, until the water is absorbed, about 18 minutes.

2. Remove from the heat and let rest, covered, for 5 to 7 minutes, then use a fork to fluff the rice and serve.

+ Gluten-Free
+ Soy-Free
+ Sugar-Free
+ Vegetarian
+ Nut-Free

Cauliflower has been my favorite vegetable for over fifteen years, and in addition to serving it on its own as a side dish, I also use it as a healthy, low-carb substitute for high-carb ingredients like rice and pasta.

CAULIFLOWER RICE WITH HERBS

INGREDIENTS

1 large head cauliflower (about 16 ounces), cut into florets

2 tablespoons extra-virgin olive oil

1/3 cup thinly chopped scallions, both white and green parts

1 garlic clove, minced

1/4 cup thinly chopped fresh parsley

1/4 cup thinly chopped fresh cilantro

1/2 teaspoon sea salt

1/2 teaspoon freshly ground black pepper

Juice of 1/2 lemon, optional

DIRECTIONS

1. Place the cauliflower in a large food processor and pulse until it is broken down into rice-sized pieces.

2. Heat the oil in a large skillet over medium-high heat. Add the scallions and garlic and cook, stirring, for 2 minutes. Stir in the riced cauliflower and cook, stirring, for 5 minutes more.

3. Remove from the heat, season with the parsley, cilantro, salt, pepper, and lemon juice, if using, and serve.

+ Gluten-Free
+ Grain-Free
+ Soy-Free
+ Sugar-Free
+ Nut-Free
+ Plant-Based

Active time: 5 minutes
Total time: 1 hour 15 minutes
Serves: 4

BLACK RICE WITH HERBS

INGREDIENTS

1 cup black rice

2 cups water

2 tablespoons olive oil

Pinch of sea salt

2 tablespoons finely chopped chives

2 tablespoons finely chopped cilantro

2 tablespoons finely chopped dill

2 tablespoons apple cider vinegar

DIRECTIONS

1. Rinse the rice, then soak in water for 30 minutes.

2. Bring the water to a boil in a small saucepan. Drain the rice and stir into the boiling water, then add 1 tablespoon of the oil and the salt.

3. Lower the heat and simmer, covered, until the water is absorbed, 35 to 40 minutes.

4. Remove from the heat and let rest, covered, for 7 to 10 minutes, then use a fork to fluff the rice. Stir in the chives, cilantro, dill, vinegar, and the remaining 1 tablespoon of oil before serving.

+ Gluten-Free
+ Soy-Free
+ Sugar-Free
+ Plant-based
+ Nut-Free

Active time: 5 minutes
Total time: 25 minutes
Serves: 4

BUCKWHEAT WITH GHEE

INGREDIENTS

1 cup roasted buckwheat

1 1/2 cups water

3 tablespoons ghee

1/2 teaspoon salt, or more to taste

DIRECTIONS

1. Rinse and drain the buckwheat. Bring the water to a boil in a small saucepan. Add the buckwheat, ghee, and salt.

2. Lower the heat and simmer, covered, until the water is absorbed, about 15 minutes.

3. Remove from the heat and let rest, covered, for 5 to 7 minutes, then use a fork to fluff and serve.

+ Gluten-Free
+ Soy-Free
+ Sugar-Free
+ Nut-Free
+ Vegetarian

Active time: 5 minutes
Total time: 25 minutes
Serves: 4

QUINOA WITH LEMON JUICE

INGREDIENTS

2 cups water

1 cup sprouted quinoa

2 tablespoons ghee

Juice of 1 small lemon

1/4 teaspoon sea salt

DIRECTIONS

1. Bring the water to a boil in a small saucepan. Add the quinoa, ghee, lemon juice, and salt.

2. Lower the heat and simmer, covered, until the water is absorbed, about 15 minutes.

3. Remove from the heat and let rest, covered, for 3 to 5 minutes, then use a fork to fluff and serve.

+ Gluten-Free
+ Soy-Free
+ Sugar-Free
+ Vegetarian
+ Nut-Free

Active time: 5 minutes
Total timw: 55 minutes
Serves: 4

BROWN RICE WITH WALNUTS

INGREDIENTS

1 cup long-grain brown rice

2 cups water

1/2 teaspoon salt

3 tablespoons olive oil

1 medium yellow onion, chopped

1 garlic clove, minced

1/2 cup chopped walnuts

DIRECTIONS

1. Rinse the rice. Bring the water to a boil in a small saucepan, then add the rice and salt.

2. Lower the heat and simmer, covered, until the water is absorbed, about 45 minutes. Remove from the heat and let rest, covered, for 5 to 7 minutes, then use a fork to fluff the rice.

3. Meanwhile, heat the oil in a large skillet over medium heat. Add the onion, garlic, and walnuts and cook, stirring, until the onions are golden, 3 to 5 minutes.

4. Spoon the cooked rice into the skillet on top of the onion-walnut mixture, mix until well combined, and serve.

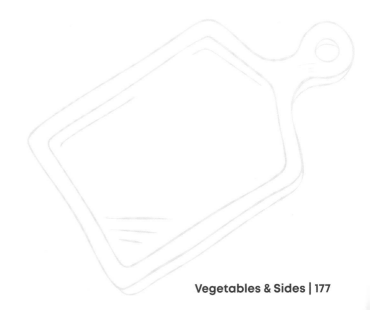

+ Gluten-Free
+ Soy-Free
+ Sugar-Free
+ Plant-Based

Active time: 10 minutes
Total time: 30 minutes
Makes: 12 cookies

Chocolate Brownie Cookies are rich in flavor and very . . . well . . . chocolatey! Made with cacao powder, they are soft and chewy with a crunchy outer shell. Whether you're a born chocolate lover or just having a chocolate craving, these cookies will not disappoint. They are tasty and easy to prepare. Enjoy!

CHOCOLATE BROWNIE COOKIES

INGREDIENTS

1 1/4 cups coconut sugar

1/2 cup cacao powder

2 tablespoons ground flaxseed

1/2 teaspoon baking soda

1/2 cup coconut oil, melted

1/2 cup almond milk

1 tablespoon vanilla extract

2 cups tigernut flour

1/2 cup shredded coconut

1/2 cup semisweet chocolate chunks

DIRECTIONS

1. Preheat the oven to 350°F. Line a baking sheet with parchment paper, or grease with coconut oil and dust with flour.

2. In a large mixing bowl, combine the coconut sugar, cacao powder, flaxseed, baking soda, melted coconut oil, almond milk, and vanilla extract and mix with a large spoon or electric mixer until smooth. Add the tigernut flour and mix again until combined. Add the shredded coconut and chocolate chunks and fold in with your hands or a spoon until evenly mixed.

3. Use a tablespoon to create evenly shaped cookies, or form the cookies by hand: Spray baking oil onto your hands, then form tablespoon-sized balls of dough and flatten with your palms. Place the cookies on the prepared baking sheet, leaving 1 to 2 inches of space between them.

4. Bake for 20 minutes. Let cool on the baking sheet for 3 to 5 minutes. Transfer cookies to a cooling rack or a room-temperature plate, and let cool for an additional 10 minutes before serving.

+ Gluten-Free
+ Grain-Free
+ Refined Sugar-Free,
+ Plant-Based
+ Soy-Free (Option)

Active time: 10 minutes
Total time: 30 minutes
Makes: 12 cookies

Chewy Almond Butter Pecan Cookies make for a perfect healthy breakfast or dessert, especially when you have a limited amount of time. Sweetened with maple syrup, this recipe is straightforward and requires minimal preparation. Throw the cookies in the oven and voilà, the results are heavenly!

With a soft and tender inside and a lightly crispy shell, these cookies are a family favorite. They're filled with wholesome and nutritious ingredients, so you can savor their distinctive rich, savory almond flavor guilt-free.

CHEWY ALMOND BUTTER PECAN COOKIES

INGREDIENTS

1 cup almond butter, at room temperature

1 cup maple syrup

1/2 teaspoon baking soda

2 3/4 cups tigernut flour

1 cup chopped pecans

DIRECTIONS

1. Preheat the oven to 350°F. Line a large baking sheet with parchment paper, or grease with coconut oil and dust with tigernut flour.

2. In a large mixing bowl, combine the almond butter, maple syrup, and baking soda. Mix the ingredients together with a spoon until smooth (if your almond butter is still cold, this step will take extra time and effort). Add the tigernut flour and continue to stir until fully combined. Stir in the chopped pecans.

3. Use a 2-tablespoon cookie scoop to form equal sized balls of dough, or use your hands to roll 2-tablespoon-sized balls and flatten with your palms. Place onto the prepared baking sheet, leaving 1 to 2 inches of space between each cookie.

4. Bake for 16 minutes, or until lightly browned. Let the cookies cool on the baking sheet for 5 minutes. Transfer to a cooling rack or a room-temperature plate and let cool for 10 more minutes before serving.

+ Gluten-Free
+ Grain-Free
+ Refined Sugar-Free
+ Plant-Based
+ Soy-Free

Active time: 10 minutes
Total time: 30 minutes
Makes: 12 cookies

These cookies are highly nutritious and grain-free, while still being delightfully rich in flavor and soft and chewy in texture. I often spread additional nut butter or regular butter on top of these cookies and enjoy them for breakfast. These power cookies are as nutritious as a good bowl of breakfast granola.

SUNFLOWER BUTTER COOKIES

INGREDIENTS

1 cup sunflower butter, at room temperature

1 cup maple syrup

1/2 teaspoons baking soda

2 3/4 cups tigernut flour or almond flour

1 cup raisins

DIRECTIONS

1. Preheat the oven to 350°F. Line a large baking sheet with parchment paper, or grease with coconut oil and dust with flour.

2. Combine the sunflower butter, maple syrup, and baking soda in a bowl and mix with a large mixing spoon or mixer until the consistency is smooth. Add the flour and continue to mix until well combined. Stir in the raisins and mix with your hands or a spoon until evenly distributed.

3. Drop about 2 tablespoons of dough per cookie onto the prepared baking sheet, spacing the cookies at least 2 inches apart, and flatten with a fork. Or use your hands to form the cookies: Form 2-tablespoon-sized balls of dough between your hands, place them on the baking sheet, and flatten with your palms.

4. Bake for 18 minutes, or until lightly browned. Let cool on the baking sheet for about 35 minutes. Transfer the cookies to a cooling rack or a room-temperature plate and let cool for 10 minutes more before serving.

+ Gluten-Free
+ Grain-Free
+ Refined Sugar-Free
+ Plant-Based
+ Soy-Free

Active time: 10 minutes
Total time: 30 minutes
Makes: 12 cookies

Although all my cookie recipes are easy to follow, these Peanut Butter and Jelly Cookies take the cake (or "take the cookie"!) for requiring the least amount of effort to prepare. In addition to being satisfyingly sweet and salty, these cookies are also jam-packed with nourishing ingredients. I love eating them for breakfast and never feel guilty. Life is all about balance, right?

PEANUT BUTTER AND JELLY COOKIES

INGREDIENTS

1 cup creamy peanut butter

1 cup maple syrup

1/2 teaspoon baking soda

2 3/4 cups tigernut flour or almond flour

1/4 cup your favorite jam

DIRECTIONS

1. Preheat the oven to 350°F. Line a large baking sheet with parchment paper, or grease with vegan butter and dust with flour.

2. Combine the peanut butter, maple syrup, and baking soda in a bowl and stir until smooth. Add the tigernut flour and mix with electric mixer or spoon until the batter is well combined.

3. Use a 2-tablespoon cookie scoop to form equal-sized balls of dough and place them on the prepared baking sheet, or use your hands to form the cookies: Spray baking oil onto your hands, then roll 2-tablespoon-sized balls of dough and place them on the baking sheet, leaving at least 2 inches of space between cookies. Press the center of each cookie with the handle end of a spoon or your thumb. Spoon 1/2 teaspoon of jam into the center indentation of each cookie.

4. Bake for 16 to 18 minutes, or until the edges are golden brown. Let cool on the baking sheet for 10 minutes. Once the cookies are beginning to set and are able to be moved, transfer to a cooling rack or a room-temperature plate. Allow the cookies to cool completely, 10 to 20 minutes more, before serving.

+ Gluten-Free
+ Grain-Free
+ Refined Sugar-Free
+ Plant-Based
+ Soy-Free

Active time: 10 minutes
Total time: 30 minutes
Makes: 12 large cookies

These cookies are mouth-watering, wholesome, and easy to prepare! Throw together a few healthy ingredients in a bowl, follow a few simple steps, and "ta da!"—the results are always successful. With a buttery, sweet, and soft taste, this cookie provides a new twist on the classic chocolate chip cookie.

COCONUT BUTTER CHOCOLATE CHIP COOKIES

INGREDIENTS

1 cup coconut butter

1 cup maple syrup

2 1/2 cups tigernut flour

1 cup dark chocolate chips

DIRECTIONS

1. Preheat the oven to 350°F. Line a large baking sheet with parchment paper, or grease with coconut butter and lightly dust with flour.

2. In a large mixing bowl, whisk together the coconut butter and maple syrup. Add the tigernut flour and whisk until well combined. Fold in the chocolate chips until they are evenly distributed.

3. Use a cookie scoop or a spoon to drop tablespoonfuls of dough onto the prepared baking sheet, or form tablespoon-sized balls of dough with your hands and place on the baking sheet, spacing them 2 inches apart.

4. Bake for 18 minutes or until lightly browned. Transfer the cookies to a cooling rack or a room-temperature plate, and cool for 15 minutes more before serving.

+ Gluten-Free
+ Grain-Free
+ Refined Sugar-Free,
+ Plant-Based
+ Soy-Free (Option)

Active time: 15 minutes
Total time: 30 minutes
Makes: 12 cookies

Pine nuts are highly nutritious and extremely versatile, making them an easy addition to any diet. They are an especially excellent ingredient for cookies, as they retain both their delicious taste and their nutritional value when baked. Enjoy these Pine Nut Cookies as a between-meals snack or as a delicious supplement to any meal!

PINE NUT COOKIES

INGREDIENTS

1 cup creamy cashew butter

1 cup maple syrup

1 tablespoon lemon zest

1/2 teaspoon baking soda

2 1/2 cups tigernut flour

1 cup pine nuts

DIRECTIONS

1. Preheat the oven to 350°F. Line a large baking sheet with parchment paper, or grease with coconut oil and lightly dust with flour.

2. In a large mixing bowl, whisk together the cashew butter, maple syrup, lemon zest, and baking soda. Add the tigernut flour and continue to whisk briskly until well combined.

3. Place the pine nuts in a shallow bowl. Spray your hands lightly with cooking oil. Scoop one tablespoon of dough per cookie and use your hands to shape the dough into 1-inch balls. Drop each ball into the pine nuts and roll it to coat with nuts, then roll the dough between your palms, pressing in the pine nuts as you go along. Arrange the cookies on the prepared baking sheet, spacing them at least 2 inches apart.

4. Bake for 15 minutes or until the edges of the cookies are golden brown. Remove from the oven and let cool on the baking sheet until they are set enough to move, 10 to 15 minutes. Transfer the cookies to a cooling rack or a room-temperature plate and let cool completely, about 15 minutes more, before serving.

+ Gluten-Free
+ Grain-Free
+ Plant-Based
+ Refined Sugar-free
+ Soy-Free

Active time: 15 minutes
Total time: 30 minutes
Makes: 15 cookies

These cookies are soft and chewy on the inside, while the outside is covered completely with crunchy sesame seeds that taste even better when baked. They are not only irresistible in taste, but also in scent—I always look forward to the aroma of toasted sesame seeds emanating from the cookies when they first come out of the oven.

SESAME COOKIES

INGREDIENTS

1 cup pumpkin puree

1/2 cup coconut oil

1 large egg

3/4 cup coconut sugar, divided

1 1/2 teaspoons baking soda

2 tablespoons ground cinnamon

1 teaspoon ground ginger

1/2 teaspoon ground nutmeg

1/2 teaspoon ground cloves

2 cups tigernut flour

3/4 cup sesame seeds

DIRECTIONS

1. Preheat the oven to 350°F. Line a baking sheet with parchment paper, or grease with coconut oil and dust with flour.

2. In a large mixing bowl, whisk together the pumpkin puree, coconut oil, egg, 1/2 cup of the coconut sugar, the baking soda, cinnamon, ginger, nutmeg, and cloves until well combined. Add the tigernut flour and continue whisking until smooth. In a separate bowl or on a plate, combine the remaining 1/4 cup of coconut sugar with the sesame seeds and mix until well combined.

3. Scoop one tablespoon of dough per cookie and use your hands to roll into individual balls. Roll each ball around in the coconut sugar/sesame seed mixture until evenly covered. Shake off any excess and place each cookie on the prepared baking sheet, spacing them 1 to 2 inches apart.

4. Bake for 15 to 20 minutes, or until the edges are golden brown. Remove from the oven and let cool on the baking sheet for 3 to 5 minutes, or until set enough to move. Transfer the cookies to a cooling rack or a room-temperature plate and let cool completely, 5 to 10 minutes more.

+ Gluten-Free
+ Grain-Free
+ Refined Sugar-Free
+ Soy-Free
+ Vegetarian
+ Dairy-free

Active time: 10 minutes
Total time: 25 minutes
Makes: 12 cookies

These make the perfect afternoon tea cookies. Matcha has so many benefits and is packed with antioxidants. It is a truly magical ingredient that boosts your metabolism and spikes your energy levels. Eat and enjoy.

MATCHA TEA COOKIES

INGREDIENTS

1 cup coconut butter

1/2 cup maple syrup

1/4 cup matcha powder

1 tablespoon vanilla extract

3/4 cup tigernut flour

DIRECTIONS

1. Preheat the oven to 350°F. Line a baking sheet with parchment paper, or grease with coconut oil and dust with tigernut flour.

2. In a large mixing bowl, combine the coconut butter, maple syrup, matcha powder, and vanilla extract and mix with electric mixer or spoon until well combined. Add the tigernut flour and mix until smooth.

3. Use a cookie scoop or a spoon to drop tablespoonfuls of dough onto the prepared baking sheet, or form tablespoon-sized balls of dough with your hands and place on the baking sheet, spacing them 2 inches apart.

4. Bake for 15 minutes, or until lightly browned. Remove from the oven and let cool on the baking sheet for 5 minutes, or until set enough to move. Transfer the cookies to a cooling rack or a room-temperature plate and let cool completely, about 10 minutes more.

+ Gluten-Free
+ Grain-Free
+ Refined Sugar-Free
+ Plant-Based
+ Soy-Free

Active time: 10 minutes
Total time: 25 minutes
Makes: 12 cookies

These irresistible cookies are like a cross between banana bread and peanut butter, and are perfect for starting your day on a sweet note. Who can say no to cookies for breakfast?

PEANUT BUTTER-BANANA COOKIES

INGREDIENTS

2 ripe bananas, peeled and mashed

1/3 cup peanut butter

1/4 cup maple syrup or agave syrup

2 teaspoons cinnamon

1/2 teaspoon baking soda

3/4 cup tigernut flour

DIRECTIONS

1. Preheat the oven to 350°F. Line a baking sheet with parchment paper, or grease with coconut oil and dust with tigernut flour.

2. In a large bowl, combine the bananas, peanut butter, maple syrup, cinnamon, and baking soda and mix with a spoon or electric mixer until smooth. Add the tigernut flour and mix until completely combined.

3. Use a cookie scoop or a spoon to drop tablespoonfuls of dough onto the prepared baking sheet, or form tablespoon-sized balls of dough with your hands and place on the baking sheet, spacing them 1 to 2 inches apart. Flatten each ball with the palm of your hand.

4. Bake for 15 minutes, or until light brown. Remove from the oven and let cool on the baking sheet for 5 minutes, or until set enough to move. Transfer to a cooling rack or room-temperature plate and let cool for 10 minutes more before serving.

+ Gluten-Free
+ Grain-Free
+ Refined Sugar-Free
+ Plant-Based
+ Soy-Free

Active time: 10 minutes
Total time: 25 minutes
Makes: 12 cookies

I love the smell of lavender and always have some in my room. If you are looking to try cookies that are a little different from the same old favorites, look no further than this recipe. Made with dried lavender and a touch of lemon, these cookies are soft in texture and exquisite in taste.

LAVENDER–LEMON ZEST COOKIES WITH CHOCOLATE DRIZZLE

INGREDIENTS

1/4 cup natural unsweetened applesauce

1/4 cup coconut oil

1/2 cup maple sugar or coconut sugar

1 tablespoon ground chia seeds

1 tablespoon ground flaxseed

1 teaspoon ground lavender

1/2 teaspoon baking soda

1/2 teaspoon ground vanilla beans or vanilla extract

1 large pinch of finely grated lemon zest

1 small pinch of sea salt

1 1/2 cups tigernut flour

1 ounce dairy-free chocolate, sweetened with coconut sugar

DIRECTIONS

1. Preheat the oven to 350°F. Line a baking sheet with parchment paper, or grease with coconut oil and dust with tigernut flour.

2. In a large mixing bowl, whisk together the applesauce, coconut oil, maple or coconut sugar, chia seeds, flaxseed, lavender, baking soda, vanilla, lemon zest, and salt until well combined. Add the tigernut flour and whisk until smooth.

3. Use a cookie scoop or a spoon to drop tablespoonfuls of dough onto the prepared baking sheet and flatten them with the back of the spoon, or spray your hands with cooking oil, roll tablespoon-sized balls of dough with your hands, flatten each ball between your palms, and place on the baking sheet, spacing the cookies 2 inches apart.

4. Bake for 14 to 16 minutes, or until lightly browned. Allow the cookies to cool on the baking sheet for 3 minutes. Transfer to a cooling rack or a room-temperature plate and let cool completely, 5 to 10 minutes more.

5. Meanwhile, heat the chocolate in a double boiler over low heat just until fully melted. Drizzle chocolate glaze over the cooled cookies. Let cool for 5 minutes before serving.

+ Gluten-Free
+ Grain-Free
+ Refined Sugar-Free
+ Plant-Based
+ Soy-Free

Active time: 20 minutes
Total time: 2 hours
Makes: 16 bars

These chocolate caramel bars are the tastiest bars I have ever made. The stylist I worked with for this book tried one during our photo shoot and loved it so much he actually reached out to me afterward asking for the recipe. I told him I was happy to share it with him—just as I'm happy to share it with all of you, through this book!

CHOCOLATE CARAMEL BARS

INGREDIENTS

FOR THE CRUST:

1/2 cup coconut oil

1/4 cup maple syrup

1 1/2 cups tigernut flour

1 tablespoon flaxseed meal

FOR THE DATE "CARAMEL":

2 cups chopped dates

1 tablespoon coconut oil

1 tablespoon vanilla extract

FOR THE CHOCOLATE COATING:

1 (4-ounce) vegan dark chocolate bar, roughly chopped

1/2 teaspoon coconut oil

1/2 teaspoon maple syrup

+ Gluten-Free
+ Grain-Free
+ Refined Sugar-Free
+ Plant-Based
+ Soy-Free

DIRECTIONS

1. Preheat the oven to 350°F. Line the bottom of a 9-x-9-inch square baking pan with parchment paper, then grease the parchment paper with coconut oil.

2. To make the crust: In a large bowl, combine the coconut oil and maple syrup together with a spoon, or blend in a food processor until smooth. Add the tigernut flour and flaxseed and stir until the mixture forms a dough.

3. Press the dough evenly into the bottom of the prepared pan and bake for 14 to 15 minutes, or until the edges are a deep golden brown and the middle is lightly golden. Press down any bubbles or spots that rise, and let the crust cool for 20 to 30 minutes before starting the caramel topping. Leave the oven on for the next step.

4. To make the date caramel: Place the chopped dates on a cookie sheet and bake for 3 to 4 minutes, or until they become soft. Transfer the hot dates to a small food processor and puree until the dates are smooth and creamy. With the food processor still running, add the coconut oil and vanilla extract. (The mixture should form a paste; add 1 to 2 tablespoons of hot water if it's too thick.) Continue to mix until well combined.

5. Once the crust has finished cooling, gently spread the date caramel evenly on top, making sure to not break the crust. Place the pan in the refrigerator until the caramel is hard, at least 20 to 25 minutes.

6. To make the chocolate coating: Once the caramel has completely hardened, melt the chocolate in a small pan or double boiler over low heat. Add the coconut oil and maple syrup and mix well until smooth. Pour the melted chocolate over the date topping and use the spoon to spread it out evenly. Place the pan back in the refrigerator until the chocolate is hard, about one hour. Once the chocolate is set, use the parchment paper to lift the bars out of the pan and slice into 16 pieces.

Active time: 15 minutes
Total time: 30 minutes
Makes: 18

I have had a sweet tooth from a very young age. These coconut truffles remind me of my childhood favorite—Sweet Treat. These make tasty holiday treats . . . but sometimes, every day is a holiday!

COCONUT TRUFFLE COOKIES

INGREDIENTS

1 cup maple syrup

1 cup coconut butter

1/4 teaspoon baking soda

2 1/2 cups tigernut flour

3/4 cup shredded coconut

DIRECTIONS

1. Preheat the oven to 350°F. Line a large baking sheet with parchment paper, or grease with coconut butter and dust with tigernut flour.

2. In a large mixing bowl, whisk together the maple syrup, coconut butter, and baking soda until thoroughly combined. Add the tigernut flour and whisk until smooth. Place the shredded coconut on a separate plate or in a shallow bowl.

3. Scoop 1 tablespoon of dough per cookie and use your hands to roll into balls, then roll each ball in the shredded coconut. Place on the prepared pan, spacing the cookies at least 2 inches apart.

4. Bake for 15 minutes, or until lightly browned. Let cool on the baking sheet for about 5 minutes, or until set enough to move. Transfer the cookies to a cooling rack or a room-temperature plate and let cool completely, about 15 minutes more, before serving.

+ Gluten-Free
+ Grain-Free
+ Refined Sugar-Free
+ Plant-Based
+ Soy-Free

Active time: 15 minutes
Total time: 1 hour
Serves: 12

This moist and delicious grain-free cake is made from fresh peaches, and is a perfect treat for special occasions and holidays. It has become a tradition in my family for me to make peach cakes every fall.

PEACH UPSIDE-DOWN CAKE

INGREDIENTS

Coconut sugar, for sprinkling

2 cups sliced peeled fresh peaches

3/4 cup maple syrup

1/2 cup coconut oil

1/2 cup unsweetened applesauce

1/4 cup hot water

2 tablespoons vanilla extract

2 1/2 cups tigernut flour

1/4 cup tapioca flour

1 tablespoon arrowroot powder

1 tablespoon ground flaxseed

1 tablespoon ground chia seed

1 teaspoon aluminum-free baking powder

1/2 teaspoon baking soda

1 cup chopped walnuts

DIRECTIONS

1. Preheat the oven to 350°F. Grease a 9-inch round baking pan with a generous amount of coconut oil and sprinkle with coconut sugar. Arrange the peach slices in a single layer over the sugar.

2. In a large bowl, whisk together the maple syrup, coconut oil, applesauce, hot water, and vanilla extract. In another bowl, combine the tigernut flour, tapioca flour, arrowroot powder, flaxseed, chia seed, baking powder, and baking soda and stir to mix.

3. Pour the dry ingredients into the wet ingredients and mix until smooth with a spoon or electric mixer. Fold in the chopped walnuts and mix with a spoon until evenly distributed. Spoon the batter over the peach slices.

4. Bake for 45 to 50 minutes, or until a toothpick inserted in the center comes out clean. Let set in the pan for about 10 minute before inverting onto a serving plate.

+ Gluten-Free
+ Grain-Free
+ Refined Sugar-Free
+ Plant-Based
+ Soy-Free

This mousse is fluffy, light, chocolatey, and delicious; perfect for satisfying any chocolate craving. Some recipes combine unexpected ingredients to yield magical results, and this is one of them.

AVOCADO CHOCOLATE MOUSSE

INGREDIENTS

2 ripe avocados, peel and pits removed

2 ripe bananas, peeled

13 Medjool dates, pitted

1/3 cup almond butter

6 tablespoons cacao powder

1/2 cup dairy-free milk

1 tablespoon vanilla extract

OPTIONAL TOPPINGS:
Shredded coconut
Sunflower seeds
Poppy seeds
Chia seeds

DIRECTIONS

1. Combine the avocado flesh, bananas, dates, almond butter, cacao powder, milk, and vanilla extract in a food processor and pulse until smooth. Divide the mixture among 6 bowls or glasses and sprinkle each serving with your favorite toppings, if using.

+ Gluten-Free
+ Grain-Free
+ Refined Sugar-Free
+ Plant-Based
+ Soy-Free

Active time: 10 minutes
Total time: 1 hour 10 minutes
Serves: 8

Seriously, you just have to make these brownies. They are perfectly sweet and satisfying: healthy and delicious, with no baking required. And they can be prepared ahead and kept in the freezer, making them an ideal dessert for your next dinner party.

RAW BROWNIES

INGREDIENTS

1 1/2 cups tigernut flour

20 Medjool dates, pitted, soaked, and drained

1/4 cup cacao powder

1 cup chopped walnuts, divided

1/2 cup coconut oil

2 tablespoons vanilla extract

DIRECTIONS

1. Combine the tigernut flour, dates, cacao powder, 1/2 cup of the walnuts, the coconut oil, and vanilla extract in a food processor. Puree until well blended.

2. Once the mixture is fully combined and very sticky, transfer it to a baking sheet and spread it to your desired thickness. Sprinkle the remaining 1/2 cup walnuts evenly over the top.

3. Freeze the brownies until fully set and very firm, about 1 hour, depending on thickness, then store them in the fridge. Slice into 8 brownies and enjoy.

+ Gluten-Free
+ Grain-Free
+ Refined Sugar-Free
+ Plant-Based
+ Soy-free
+ Raw/No-Bake

Active time: 10 minutes
Total time: 40 minutes
Makes: 9 brownies

These particular baked brownies are one of my favorite desserts by far, and everyone who has ever tried this recipe has loved it. They are perfectly sweet with a slightly bittersweet chocolate flavor. They are so good that even the diehard omnivores in your life will love them.

FUDGY DOUBLE-CHOCOLATE BROWNIES

INGREDIENTS

2 1/2 cups tigernut flour

2 cups coconut sugar

1 1/2 cups cacao powder

2 tablespoons ground flaxseed

2 tablespoons ground chia seeds

1/2 teaspoon aluminum-free baking powder

1 1/2 cups dairy-free milk

1/2 cup melted coconut oil

1 tablespoon vanilla extract

1 cup vegan chocolate chunks

DIRECTIONS

1. Preheat the oven to 350°F. Line the bottom of a 9-x-9-inch square baking pan with parchment, then grease the parchment with coconut oil.

2. In a large bowl, combine the tigernut flour, coconut sugar, cacao powder, flaxseed, chia seeds, and baking powder and stir to mix. In a small bowl, whisk together the dairy-free milk, melted coconut oil, and vanilla extract. Pour the wet ingredients into the dry ingredients and whisk until smooth. Fold in the chocolate chunks until they are spread evenly throughout the batter, then spoon the batter into the prepared pan.

3. Bake for 30 minutes, or until a toothpick inserted in the center comes out clean. Let the brownies cool for 15 to 20 minutes in the pan. Carefully remove them from the pan and allow to cool completely before slicing into 9 brownies.

+ Gluten-Free
+ Grain-Free
+ Refined Sugar-Free
+ Plant-Based
+ Soy-Free

Active time: 15 minutes
Total time: 50 minutes
Serves: 6

I learned to love baked apples from my grandmother, who used to serve them with vanilla ice cream. I especially love making them during apple-picking season, when fresh, local apples are available.

BAKED APPLES

INGREDIENTS

6 sweet, medium-sized apples, such as Honeycrisp or Fuji

1 cup shredded coconut

1/3 cup chopped walnuts

1/4 cup tigernut flour

2 tablespoons hemp seeds

1/3 cup maple syrup

1/4 cup coconut oil

2 tablespoons tahini

1 tablespoon ground cinnamon

DIRECTIONS

1. Preheat the oven to 375°F. Line a baking sheet with parchment paper, or grease with coconut oil and dust with tigernut flour.

2. Use an apple corer to remove the full core from each apple, leaving the apples intact with a hole from top to bottom.

3. In a large bowl, combine the shredded coconut, walnuts, tigernut flour, hemp seeds, maple syrup, coconut oil, tahini, and cinnamon and stir to mix. Place the apples on the prepared baking sheet and stuff each apple core with the shredded coconut mix, then sprinkle all of the leftover mix around the apples.

4. Place the apples in the oven and bake for 35 minutes, or until they are completely soft. Let rest until they are your desired temperature. You can serve warm or at room temperature.

+ Gluten-Free
+ Grain-Free
+ Refined Sugar-Free
+ Soy-Free
+ Plant-Based

Active time: 20 minutes
Total time: 5 hours 30 mins
Serves: 8

This easy, grain-free pecan pie recipe deserves a place at your holiday table. This is my favorite pie, and I hope it becomes one of your favorites as well!

PECAN PIE

INGREDIENTS

FOR THE CRUST:

1/2 cup coconut oil

1/4 cup maple syrup

1 3/4 cups tigernut flour, sifted

1 tablespoon flax meal

FOR THE FILLING:

3 tablespoons ground flaxseed

8 tablespoons warm water

1 1/4 cups roughly chopped pecans

3/4 cup coconut sugar or maple sugar

1/4 cup maple syrup

2 tablespoons coconut oil

Pinch of salt

+ Gluten-Free
+ Grain-Free
+ Refined Sugar-Free
+ Soy-Free
+ Plant-Based

DIRECTIONS

1. Preheat the oven to 350°F. Line the bottom of a 9-x-9-inch baking pan with parchment, then grease the parchment with coconut oil.

2. To make the crust: In a bowl, beat the coconut oil and maple syrup together with a large spoon until well combined. Add the tigernut flour and flax meal and stir until a dough is formed. Press the dough evenly into the bottom of the prepared pan.

3. Bake for 14 to 15 minutes, or until the edges are a deep golden brown and the middle is lightly golden. Let cool for 1 hour before filling. Leave the oven on for the pecans.

4. To make the filling: As soon as the crust comes out of the oven, whisk the ground flaxseed with the warm water and refrigerate for at least 20 minutes to make flax eggs.

5. Meanwhile, place the chopped pecans on a cookie sheet and bake until they begin to smell nutty, about 8 minutes. Set aside.

6. Once the crust has cooled, combine the coconut sugar, maple syrup, coconut oil, and salt in a large saucepan over high heat and bring to a boil. Lower the heat to medium and boil for about 1 minute, stirring frequently, then remove from the heat. Let stand at room temperature for 5 minutes, then add the chilled flax eggs and mix well. Stir in the chopped pecans.

7. Pour the filling over the crust and use a spoon to spread it out evenly, making sure the pecans lay flat. Bake until the filling looks set, about 20 minutes. Cool to room temperature, then refrigerate for at least 4 hours or overnight. Once the pie is fully chilled, slice and serve cold.

Total time: 5 minutes
Makes: enough to frost 12
cupcakes

LEMON-VANILLA FROSTING

INGREDIENTS

1 1/2 cups unsweetened Tigernut Milk (page 62), or any dairy-free milk

1/4 cup maple syrup or agave nectar

1 tablespoon vanilla extract

3/4 cup coconut milk powder

1 tablespoon coconut flour

1 1/2 cups coconut oil

2 tablespoons fresh lemon juice

DIRECTIONS

1. In a blender or a food processor, combine the tigernut milk, maple syrup, vanilla extract, coconut milk powder, and coconut flour. Blend the ingredients for 2 minutes, then, with the machine running on the lowest setting, add the coconut oil and lemon juice.

2. Use the frosting immediately, or transfer to an airtight container and refrigerate for up to 6 days.

+ Gluten-Free
+ Grain-Free
+ Refined Sugar-Free
+ Soy-Free
+ Plant-Based

Total time: 5 minutes, plus
chilling time
Makes 1 1/2 cups, enough to
frost 12 cupcakes

This quick, plant-based recipe makes a homemade whipped cream that is rich and creamy. It is a great topping for pies and ice cream and perfect for frosting cupcakes and cakes.

WHIPPED COCONUT CREAM

INGREDIENTS

1 (13.5-ounce) can coconut cream, chilled in the can overnight

2 tablespoons honey or maple syrup or powdered maple sugar

1/2 teaspoon vanilla extract, optional

DIRECTIONS

1. Chill a large mixing bowl for at least 15 minutes before beginning the recipe. Open the can of chilled coconut cream, carefully spoon the thickened cream from the top, and place it in the chilled bowl, leaving the liquid behind. (You can save the liquid for use in smoothies or other recipes.)

2. Whip the coconut cream with an electric mixer on medium speed until smooth, about 1 minute. Add the sweetener and vanilla extract, if using, and whip for 1 minute more.

3. Serve immediately or refrigerate for up to 5 days in an airtight container.

+ Gluten-Free
+ Grain-Free
+ Refined Sugar-Free
+ Soy-Free
+ Plant-Based

Active time: 10 minutes
Total time: 35 minutes
Makes: 12 cupcakes

This is my go-to vanilla cupcake recipe—they are soft, fluffy, sweet, and perfect for any special occasion. For a vegan version, you can replace the regular eggs with flax eggs. You can top them with any nut butter or vanilla frosting.

VANILLA CUPCAKES

INGREDIENTS

3 large eggs, or 3 flax eggs

1 1/4 cups tigernut flour

3/4 cup coconut sugar

1/4 cup coconut flour

1/4 cup arrowroot flour

1 teaspoon baking soda

3/4 cup water

1/3 cup melted coconut oil

2 tablespoons vanilla extract

Pinch of salt

Lemon-Vanilla Frosting (page 216) or Whipped Coconut Cream (page 217), for topping

DIRECTIONS

1. Preheat the oven to 350°F. Line a 12-cup muffin tin with cupcake liners.
For the vegan version, create 3 flax eggs by mixing 3 tablespoons flaxseed meal and 9 tablespoons water; transfer to the fridge and let rest for 15 to 30 minutes to thicken.

2. In a large bowl, combine the eggs or flax eggs, tigernut flour, coconut sugar, coconut flour, arrowroot flour, baking soda, water, coconut oil, vanilla extract, and salt and whisk together until smooth.

3. Pour the batter into the prepared pan to fill each cup three-quarters full. Bake for 25 minutes for the regular version, or 35 minutes for the vegan version. Let cool in the pan for about ten minutes. Remove cupcakes from the pan and let cool completely on a rack before frosting.

+ Gluten-Free
+ Grain-Free
+ Refined Sugar-Free
+ Soy-Free
+ Dairy-Free
+ Vegetarian

Active time: 10 minutes
Total time: 30 minutes
Makes: 12 protein balls

HEMP SEED PROTEIN BALLS

INGREDIENTS

8 Medjool dates, pitted

1/2 cup sliced tigernuts, toasted for 10 minutes

1/2 cup chopped walnuts, toasted for 10 minutes

2 tablespoons coconut oil

1 teaspoon ground cinnamon

Pinch of ground cloves

Pinch of ground nutmeg

Pinch of salt

2 tablespoons hemp seeds

DIRECTIONS

1. Combine the dates, tigernuts, walnuts, coconut oil, cinnamon, cloves, nutmeg, and salt in the bowl of a food processor and process until well combined. If the mixture seems too dry add a bit more olive oil. Place the hemp seeds on a plate or in a shallow bowl.

2. Scoop tablespoon-sized portions of dough and squeeze tightly in the palm of your hand, then roll each into a small ball shape, about 1 inch in diameter. Roll each ball in the hemp seeds to coat.

3. Chill for at least 20 minutes before serving.

4. Store in an airtight container in the refrigerator for up to 1 week, or in the freezer for up to 2 months.

+ Gluten-Free
+ Grain-Free
+ Refined Sugar-Free
+ Soy-Free
+ Plant-Based

Acive time: 10 minutes
Total time: 20 minutes
Makes: 12 protein balls

This is my go-to protein ball recipe. I make them every other week and keep them in the fridge to enjoy as a snack whenever I need a pick-me-up.

ENERGY PROTEIN BALLS

INGREDIENTS

1 1/2 cups tigernut flour

1/4 cup cacao powder

1/2 cup peanut butter

1/3 cup maple syrup

1/4 cup coconut oil

DIRECTIONS

1. Combine all the ingredients in a food processor and pulse until well combined. Scoop tablespoon-sized portions of dough and roll into small balls with your hands. Chill for at least 10 minutes before serving. Store in an airtight container in the refrigerator for up to 1 week, or in the freezer for up to 2 months.

+ Gluten-Free
+ Grain-Free
+ Refined Sugar-Free
+ Soy-Free
+ Plant-Based

ACKNOWLEDGMENTS

It took about two years to create this book, and many talented individuals put their heart into it. I'm so grateful for every one of you.

+ First and foremost I'd like to say thank you to my partner **George Papanastasatos.** It's hard to describe in words how much I love you and appreciate you. You have lightened up my life!! You are an entrepreneurial artist, and as we have created businesses and gone through so many challenges together, always taking risks, not being afraid to fail, and never settling for a safe and predictable path, you have constantly pushed me to expand my comfort zone. As I wrote this book you were my recipe tester, always there with an honest opinion, and during photo-shoot days you ran from one store to another to find the beautiful plates, cups, and other props to help me achieve the best photos. You were a part of those long grocery-shopping days, too, helping to gather ingredients for the recipes—so much so that we often joked that the Whole Foods store in Tribeca was our date spot. You have been the inspiration behind my journey, bringing my body back to health, and I couldn't have done it without you. I'm so grateful to have you in my life.

+ My son **Lukas Papanastasatos,** you are my all-time favorite recipe tester and my heart and soul. You have been there playing patiently with your Legos and cars while I tested recipes, and so often volunteered to shape cookies or to mix ingredients for muffins and cakes. I've seeing you developing a love for real-food baking, and there is no better reward to me than seeing your excitement over healthy, freshly homemade sweets and baked goods.

+ I would like to thank **Jarret Egan** (photography) and **Philippe Grenade** (styling). The vast majority of the recipes in this book were shot by Jarret and styled by Phillippe. We spent many weekends creating beautiful recipe and family photos, and your vibrant energy has been so motivational; I loved every moment we spent together. Jarret and Philippe, you are both amazing people and incredibly talented artists, and I'm so grateful for you and your work.

+ Thank you to graphic designer **Simone Spitzer.** You have been so patient with the countless revisions. You are a passionate artist as well as a professional, always receiving feedback without ego and genuinely striving to deliver results. It's been a pleasure working with you—I am so impressed by what a hardworking person you are, sometimes putting days of work into a single page. You clearly love what you do and it comes across in your work!

✚ To my brilliant editor **Christine,** thank you for contributing your passion, expertise, and pure enthusiasm to this book. I'm so thankful our paths have crossed and that I was able to work with you—and was so flattered to learn that working on this book inspired you to add some of my favorite ingredients to your pantry!

✚ To my dearest friend **Adi Ortner,** thank you for the constant encouragement. For the past fifteen years you have been there to support me during any struggle I encountered, personally and professionally. Thank you for tutoring me throughout my college days, for proofreading and editing the very first draft of this book—what a challenge!—and for always believing in me.

✚ And finally, thank you to my amazing friend **Pooja Malani** and wonderful photographer.

INDEX

ABOUT THE AUTHOR

Mariam Kinkladze is a Columbia University graduate, majoring in Political Science. She is an entrepreneur and co-founder of a food and beverage company, introducing the tigernut root through an array of products to the United States market. Mariam is a proud mother, recipe creator and lover of nature. She enjoys daily yoga exercises and spending time with her family, as well as living a healthy lifestyle complete with sustainably sourced foods. Cooking is Mariam's favorite hobby—she can do it all day and every day, whipping up delicious recipes for her loved ones!

Designed by MoneMedia

Photography by Jarret C. Egan & Pooja Malani
Stylist: Philippe Grenade